MW01462786

Reckless Legislation

Reckless Legislation

How Lawmakers Ignore the Constitution

Michael A. Bamberger

Rutgers University Press
New Brunswick, New Jersey, and London

Library of Congress Cataloging-in-Publication Data

Bamberger, Michael A.
    Reckless legislation : how lawmakers ignore the Constitution / Michael A. Bamberger.
       p. cm.
    Includes bibliographical references and index.
    ISBN 0-8135-2732-5 (cloth : alk. paper)
      1. Legislation—United States—Moral and ethical aspects.
  2. Legislators—United States. 3. Law and politics. I. Title.
KF4945.B36   2000
328.73'0749—dc21   99-32376
                                                                                   CIP
British Cataloging-in-Publication data for this book is available from the British Library

Copyright © 2000 by Michael A. Bamberger
All rights reserved
No part of this book may be reproduced or utilized in any form or by any means, electronic or mechanical, or by any information storage and retrieval system, without written permission from the publisher. Please contact Rutgers University Press, 100 Joyce Kilmer Avenue, Piscataway, NJ 08854-8099. The only exception to this prohibition is "fair use" as defined by U.S. copyright law.

Manufactured in the United States of America

*This book is dedicated
to the memory of my father,
Fritz Bamberger,
a scholar.*

Contents

	Acknowledgments	ix
	Introduction	1
1	A Brief Historical Overview	15
2	Children, Fear, and the Internet	35
3	The Wright Brothers' First Plane Didn't Fly Either	71
4	A Constitution-Proof Law	97
5	If At First You Don't Succeed, Try, Try Again	111
6	Legislative Reversal	141
7	Advisory Opinions and Other Proposed Remedies	167
8	Conclusion	191
	Statistical Appendix: Analysis of a Survey of Legislators, Legislative Counsels, and Offices of the Attorneys General	199
	Notes	209
	Index	227

Acknowledgments

This book was written because Marlie Wasserman, the director of Rutgers University Press, saw the seed of the topic in a comment I made while addressing a group of publishers. During the book's creation, I was ably assisted by Jeffrey Wengrofsky, who provided valuable effort and advice. Most of all, however, I have benefited greatly from the advice, criticism, and highly skilled editing of my wife, Phylis Skloot Bamberger, who also endured, without complaint, repeated vacations which I devoted in part to writing this book.

Reckless Legislation

Introduction

Article VI of the United States Constitution imposes upon every United States senator and representative, as well as all members of any state legislature, the requirement that they take an oath or affirmation to support the Constitution. The significance of this oath to the Founding Fathers is apparent. Not only is this the only specific requirement imposed on state legislators by the federal Constitution; one of the first statutes passed by the new Congress after ratification of the Constitution established the oath to be taken by federal and state legislators.[1]

Congress and all the states have established such an oath or affirmation in compliance with this constitutional mandate. Some are long and complex; some are short and sweet. State legislators are required to swear or affirm to support or uphold their respective state constitutions, as well. But what do these oaths really mean?

At some level the meaning is fairly obvious and generally accepted. The legislator must accept the basic republican principles embodied in the Constitution and the principles of the Bill of Rights, the first ten amendments to the Constitution. The legislator must not attempt to change those principles and rights except by the amendatory process set forth in the Constitution; and, most directly, the legislator must not participate in attempts to overthrow a government established in accordance with the Constitution. I propose to discuss and analyze a more complex issue raised by these oaths—the obligation of legislators to consider seriously the constitutionality or unconstitutionality of proposed legislation, rather than deferring any such consideration, or affirmatively forwarding it, for future consideration by the courts, and the impact on our system of government of legislators' disregard of this obligation. A vote by a legislator for a bill that he or she believes to be unconstitutional or perhaps even a vote for a bill when a legislator has doubts as to its constitutionality would be a violation of the oath.[2] A more difficult issue arises when a legislator in believes good faith that the Supreme Court has decided a case or series of cases wrongly; when, in the opinion of the legislator, the Supreme Court has misread the meaning of the Constitution.

I shall consider both legislative consideration and legislative avoidance of issues of constitutionality by examining a number of actual examples: Congress and two state legislatures dealing with regulation of Internet content impinging on constitutional rights; the Indianapolis City Council and the Tennessee legislature relying on "experts" to pass unconstitutional laws; the citizens of Bellingham, Washington, enacting by initiative an ordinance previously held unconstitutional by the courts; the New York and Missouri legislatures' efforts to wear down courts and the opposition by repeatedly passing unconstitutional laws involving, respectively, religion and abortion; and Congress twice attempting to reverse Supreme Court constitutional decisions, reflecting a belief that the Court's decisions were incorrect or harmful.

Until the twentieth century, resolution of conflicts between constitution and statutes was a uniquely American issue.[3] It was not an issue in England, from which the United States derives its common law heritage. In England then (and still to this day), the core documents that are the equivalent of the U.S. Constitution are considered political documents to be interpreted by Parliament, not the courts. (An additional difference between the English and American models results from the existence in the United States of an independently elected executive. Thus, in the American system there are three potential claimants to the obligation to resolve questions of legislative unconstitutionality, while there would only be two in the English system.) Before 1803, when Chief Justice Marshall, writing for a unanimous Supreme Court, held in *Marbury v. Madison* that the Court had the power to invalidate congressional acts that it found not in accord with the Constitution, it was not clear whether the courts had such a power. (For a period of time thereafter, some, including a number of the Founding Fathers, believed that the decision in *Marbury* was incorrect.)

Once it was decided that the courts had the power to strike down congressional acts for unconstitutionality, there remained the question of whether this meant that only the courts had the competence to determine this issue or whether the legislative and executive branches also bore responsibility for maintaining constitutional standards. These alternatives have been described as the "judicial monopoly theory" and the "tripartite theory."[4] Ultimately, the latter prevailed, so that the courts, the legislature, and the executive are generally each considered to have an obligation to avoid unconstitutional legislation and governmental action, though the relative roles differ in differing situations and at differing times. Nevertheless, even late in the twentieth century, legislators faced with constitutional issues but desirous of enacting the legislation at issue defer to the judiciary. When constitutional issues were raised in connection with that part of the Alaska statehood bill that permitted the federal government to withdraw substantial parts of Alaskan land from state control, Senator Henry Jackson of Washington, who favored passage of the bill, stated,

> . . . it is an inescapable fact that fifty per cent of the lawyers are wrong in every law suit.
>
> We would spend the rest of this session and all of the next arguing the legal authorities on both side of this question. But that is not the function of this body. Our function is to make a legislative decision. Do we want statehood for Alaska, or do we not?
>
> Nothing here can change the Constitution, nor is it intended to do so. Nothing is more certain in our law than the fact that state laws and the laws of Congress must conform to the Constitution as interpreted by the Supreme Court of the United States.[5]

Thus, Jackson concluded, "Whatever doubts may exist on the subject, I believe they should be resolved in favor of constitutionality." If, as these sentiments suggest, a legislator should heed the call of unconstitutionality only when the call is of unanimous voices without dissent, the role of the legislator in preventing the passage of unconstitutional legislation and the constitutional obligation of the legislator pursuant to the oath are minimal. History has demonstrated that there is always someone, often a law school professor, willing to argue the constitutionality of almost any proposal.

At times the fact that a bill is considered unconstitutional by its opponents has been twisted into an argument in favor of passage. In the debate before the Minneapolis City Council over the MacKinnon/Dworkin civil rights antipornography bill (discussed in chapter 3), the Minnesota Civil Liberties Union led the fight for those who believed the bill to be (as the courts ultimately held) unconstitutional. Charlee Hoyt, the leader of the proponents on the council, was quoted as saying, "If they (the MCLU) think it's so blasted unconstitutional and will be thrown out, then why are they fighting it so vehemently?"[6] Such an argument totally disregards the constitutional obligations of the members of the Minneapolis City Council.

Further, it is often suggested that a 5-4 decision of the Supreme Court should be given less deference than one that is unanimous. I think this position misunderstands the Supreme Court. The Court must be viewed as a corporate institution, rather than a group of nine individuals expressing individual views. While occasionally 5-4 decisions of the Court are short-lived (the flag salute cases[7] come to mind), for the most part such a decision has no less a likelihood of long life than a decision with fewer dissenters. During the debate on the Omnibus Crime Control and Safe Streets Act of 1968, discussed in chapter 6, the Senate Judiciary Committee report, in discussing the provision overruling the *Miranda*[8] decision said, "After all, the *Miranda* decision itself was by a bare majority of one, and with increasing frequency the Supreme Court has reversed itself. The committee feels that by the time the issue of constitutionality would reach the Supreme Court, the probability is that this legislation would be upheld."[9] Thirty years later, notwithstanding the four dissents and significant changes in the composition and tenor of the Court, the *Miranda* decision remains in force, except possibly in federal courts in the five states under the jurisdiction of the United States Court of Appeals for the Fourth Circuit, because in 1999 that court, by a vote of 2-1, upheld the *Miranda*-limiting provisions of the 1968 Act.[10]

The issue of judicial review raised and settled by the Court in *Marbury* was faced and similarly resolved in the various states. To a certain extent, the states' resolution was simpler and perhaps easier because it was not complicated by issues of states' rights and limited powers. Also, for the vast majority of the states that entered the Union after 1803, the *Marbury* decision and the federal experience settled the issue decidedly in favor of granting the judiciary the final word as to the meaning of the Constitution and the power to determine whether acts of the legislature conflict with the Constitution.

In recent years there has been an increasing willingness by both state and federal legislators, particularly when dealing with issues that have raised political emotions and thus carry with them risks to political careers, to pass laws disregarding constitutional violations in those laws or to dismiss doubts about constitutionality as not being their concern. This is not to say that it is always easy to determine what meets constitutional standards and what does not. Prior to judicial determination, the constitutionality of a statute, like much else in life, is often not a matter of black or white, but rather of shades of gray. The obligation of the legislator is not to be right in every case, but rather to recognize and consider constitutional issues deliberately and seriously. It is also true that in some cases alleged constitutional issues are raised—occasionally one might even say fabricated—by opponents of a particular legislative proposal. But the source of the claim of unconstitutionality should not relieve a legislator from serious consideration of the claim.

Most legislative bodies have institutional sources for legal and constitutional advice. In some states the attorney general serves that role; in others there is a separate person or body, sometimes called legislative counsel. The nature of the advisory body may affect how it is used in a politicized dispute. If the attorney general or other legal advisor is of a different political affiliation than those pushing a legislative proposal, advice as to possible unconstitutionality can be dismissed by supporters of the allegedly unconstitutional legislation as politically motivated, however accurate or well meaning the legal opinion may be. In the fight over restrictions on Missouri family planning funds, discussed in chapter 5, the attorney general was prochoice and the proponents of the restrictions were antiabortion. Not only were the proponents unwilling to rely on the attorney general's advice; they alleged that he had, in effect, sabotaged the defense of the law in the courts after passage.

Similarly, when the legal advisor is politically allied with the proponents of the legislation and issues an opinion of constitutionality, suspicions of political bias may be raised by opponents of the legislation. While having an institutional legislative legal advisor is helpful, the quality of the advice and political considerations may limit the benefits if the advisor is not trusted by the legislators as an objective nonpartisan. In the Missouri family planning appropriations conflicts discussed in chapter 5, the antiabortion legislature considered the prochoice attorney general as an adversary rather than a counselor. And, as discussed in chapter 4, the Indianapolis City Council leadership, in promoting a civil rights antipornography law, sought the advice of a sympathetic district attorney's office rather than a critical city attorney's office.

In recent years there has been an increase in the number of unconstitutional statutes passed by state and federal legislatures, resulting partly from the failure of legislators to accept their inherent responsibility as spelled out in their oaths of office. This failure to accept constitutional responsibility can often be explained as one of political expedience. At both the federal and state levels, legislators are often more susceptible to popular pressure than judges are. They are directly elected and have relatively short terms. On the other hand, federal and many state judges are appointed in a manner that attempts to remove them from direct electoral pressure: many have lifetime appointments, either by law or as a practical matter. Even when judges are elected, their terms generally exceed those of the legislators in the same jurisdiction.

Some legislators justify the failure to consider constitutional issues seriously on theoretical grounds, appealing to the "judicial monopoly" theory to legitimize their lack of constitutional concern. They state that, since the courts are the appropriate arbiters of constitutionality, it would be institutionally incorrect for legislators to take a position prior to determination by the courts. (Sometimes this is put differently, suggesting that one cannot know what is constitutional until the courts have ruled. This involves an undercurrent that constitutionality is a secret fact known only to the keepers of the legal Holy Grail—the courts— or that the courts' determination of constitutionality is like the roll of the dice, undeterminable in advance.) However, the fact that the courts are the final arbiters of constitutionality does not have to diminish the obligation of legislators to meet their constitutional obligations; nor should it do so.

This dereliction of duty by legislators is more than an abstract issue of political theory. Rather, this dereliction has had practical repercussions on American politics in the latter part of the twentieth century. Probably the most significant impact has been to politicize the courts—or at least to establish a belief in large segments of the public that the courts have been politicized—by transferring many of the most contentious political and social issues of our times to the courts for resolution in the context of constitutional litigation and then, in the event of a finding of unconstitutionality, complaining about the politicization and "judicial activism."

Conservative politicians and commentators have, since

the Warren Court of the 1960s, bemoaned what has been characterized as "judicial activism," "judicial arrogance," or "an entrenched pattern of government by judges that is nothing less than the usurpation of politics."[11] Such critics assert that courts should not apply what they see as a "liberal" constitutional ethic to the political, highly controversial issues of the day. This view has been incorporated into proposals to limit the powers of the courts,[12] to appoint judges more congenial to such a limitation, and, at the extreme, civil disobedience.[13] But interestingly enough, as we shall see, it is often the political right that spearheads the passage of laws dealing with crime, sex, and abortion with the knowledge of their unconstitutionality. It ill behooves such critics to complain when there is judicial resolution of constitutional claims; the very vehemence of the complaint diverts the attention of the polity from the substance of the disagreement to issues of institutional structure including questions of the legitimacy of the judiciary. And it is often political impasses in the legislature that lead to shifting the resolution of these difficult "political" issues to the courts.[14]

Constitutional litigation involves very different dynamics than the political process. A significant part of the political process is accommodation and compromise. Constitutional litigation, on the other hand, generally either upholds or strikes down the whole; it does not provide for an intermediate accommodation or a moderately acceptable alternative. In this sense it is a harsher and more confrontational process. In the event of a finding of unconstitutionality, the proponents of the law are left with the feeling that the legislative will—the will of the representatives of the majority—has been thwarted by fiat of judges who, in many cases, do not bear the imprimatur of popular election. If the statute is held constitutional, opponents feel that the issue has been decided, not on the merits of the proposal, but rather on the issue of its constitutionality, a different matter entirely. Shifting the issue to the judicial forum not only extends the discussion over a period of years, that being the usual timetable of constitutional litigation,[15] but also shifts the subject of the discussion away from the social or political merits of the legislation to its constitutionality.

Politicization of the judicial branch may have harmful consequences. Increasing the number of times the courts must adjudicate contentious political issues in the constitutional context increases the harm; it makes it appear that the courts are usurping legislative power. It is a reflection of this situation that late in 1996 a number of leading conservatives participated in a symposium entitled "The End of Democracy? The Judicial Usurpation of Politics."[16] Concern about this politicization has been used by some as a lever to diminish or discredit the use by the power of the courts established in *Marbury*. This would reach a curious result, if successful. The consequence of legislators' abdication of their obligation to uphold the Constitution by not passing unconstitutional laws would be a limitation or denigration of the power of the courts, the very power and prerogative that was the stated basis of the abdication.

The perception or appearance of politicization is equally harmful. It is important that citizens believe in the impartiality of the judiciary and the judicial system, the concept of equal justice for all. Contentions that the courts have been politicized work against the acceptance of such a belief.

The flip side of the real or perceived politicization of the courts has been the increasing tendency to view and frame the major political and social issues of the day in constitutional terms—as being inexorably intertwined with issues of constitutionality. Some view this with alarm; early in 1998 Justice Antonin Scalia, speaking to the leadership of the

American Medical Association, suggested that issues such as abortion rights, the death penalty, and physician-assisted suicide should be decided by the legislature on the basis of what is socially desirable, not left to the Supreme Court.[17] (This proposal is, however, somewhat unrealistic. Given the jurisprudence of the Supreme Court, a number of the likely resolutions of these issues by legislatures would be viewed by a number of justices other than Justice Scalia— perhaps even a majority—as unconstitutional. One also wonders whether Scalia would give legislatures the same free hand when dealing with issues such as regulation of hate speech, as to which Scalia has defined limits for a majority of the Court.)

On the other hand, law professors Mark Tushnet and L. Michael Seidman view this constitutionalization of social and political issues as potentially beneficial, because discussion of these issues thus relates to the "fundamental character of our country."[18] They recognize, however, that this benefit has not been achieved, since the quality of discussion between proponents and opponents in these discussions for the most part has been very poor, with each side claiming that the constitutional answer is easily determinable and obviously in their favor.

There is also a very practical impact of this legislative abdication on the protection of constitutional rights. Challenges to unconstitutional statutes are expensive; the challenge to the CDA's regulation of the Internet, discussed in chapter 2, cost well over one million dollars. A challenge that reaches the United States Supreme Court generally involves a trial or other hearing before the trial court; briefs and an oral argument before an intermediate appellate court; briefs and an oral argument before the state supreme court (if originally brought in the state court system); briefs requesting the U.S. Supreme Court to accept the case if the challenger lost in the intermediate federal or state supreme court; briefs requesting the U.S. Supreme Court not to accept the case if the challenger had been victorious; and, if the case is considered by the U.S. Supreme Court, briefs and an oral argument before that Court. The costs of such a challenge can range from hundreds of thousand dollars to one or more million dollars. The factors that impact on cost include the legal and factual complexity of the issues, whether as a tactic the case is defended in a way that is intended to maximize the cost to the challenger, and the responses of the various judges before whom the matter will be heard.

The cost of challenging the constitutionality of legislation in terms of money and time is enormous. At the same time, the defender of the allegedly unconstitutional legislation is usually (as in all the examples discussed in this book) a government or governmental agency, because the greatest number of political/constitutional issues concern the relationship between individuals and the state or the scope of the power of the state vis-à-vis its citizens. While the state and federal governments have monetary concerns, they have attorney-employees so that the financial burden of such a litigation is not readily apparent. The state or federal government will usually vigorously defend allegedly unconstitutional statutes even when the executive branch had previously opposed passage of the law, sometimes based on constitutional concerns. The theory often is that it is "the job" of the state or federal attorney general to defend the validity of all duly enacted laws.[19] When the government does not desire, for political or other reasons, to defend using government lawyers, there are usually provisions for private attorneys to be retained at government expense.

A middle ground approach is for the government to defend at the trial level only and not appeal any loss. This, for example, was the position of the Missouri attorney general with respect to the family planning restrictions, discussed in chapter 5, and of the governor of Arizona with respect to a successful challenge to a "English language only" provision added to the Arizona Constitution.[20]

Shifting the bulk of the cost of testing constitutionality to the citizenry imposes significant financial burdens, as well as social costs. The Constitution protects the less affluent as well as the well-to-do. On constitutional issues that have particular impact on the poor and dispossessed, the burden is greatest, particularly at a time of reduction in the funding and permissible scope of federally funded legal services. But there are broader issues that apply as well to those, both corporate and individual, who can afford such a challenge. For example, why should citizens be required to expend their personal resources to defend their constitutional rights against a statute passed by legislators who generally understood it to be unconstitutional, particularly when the other side is funded by the resources of "their" government? In addition, one wonders whether, in a time of increasingly competitive fiscal needs, this is a socially valuable use of governmental, private, and charitable funds.

And should individuals and groups in the private sector determine whether an unconstitutional statute should be challenged. The Kiryas Joel School Board statutes were challenged by the New York State School Boards Association. Had the association not done so, it is not clear that the laws, which had broad support, would have been important enough to any individual or group to justify the time, cost, and commitment required for the challenge.

The irresponsible passage of unconstitutional legislation leads to unhealthy cynicism and is harmful to our system of government. The unwillingness of legislators, at both the state and federal levels, to consider seriously the constitutionality of legislation when it is not politically expedient to do so constitutes an abdication of their constitutional responsibilities in the most fundamental sense: it constitutes an undermining for political and selfish motives of the system they are sworn to serve.

In the following pages I shall consider a few recent examples to provide a clearer focus on the nature of the problem and examine in greater depth the impact from a social and political viewpoint of the increasing trend of legislative abdication.

1

A Brief

Historical

Overview

The founders of the American republic designed a federal government in which the United States Constitution, by its terms, was to be the supreme law of the land. Thus, federal or state laws in conflict with the Constitution presumably are without effect because they are unconstitutional. However, neither the Constitution nor any other of the founding charter documents designate who is to determine whether a statute conflicts with that supreme law and who is to assure that the Constitution remains the controlling law.

To demonstrate some of the difficulties attending to these conflict-resolution issues, it is worthwhile to review historical arguments. The U.S. Constitution has been called many things—the Basic Law, the framework of our government, the source of our liberties and freedoms. But, without doubt, it is law. Unlike the British charter documents, it is not a political document setting forth aspirations and goals. A closer look at what the Constitution is and what it is not should be helpful in discussing how legislators can, should, and do apply it in the assessment of proposed legislation on which they must vote. A comparison of the Constitution with the Declaration of Independence highlights the issue.

The Declaration of Independence clearly is a statement of principles, goals, and morals; it was not intended to be law. The Declaration sets forth a democratic theory of government, the aims and intentions of the government of the new nation, and the rights that government should honor. The Constitution, on the other hand, describes the governmental structure through which these goals are to be effectuated. It sets forth a specific institutional structure, paying particular attention to the "hot" issues of the late 1790s that had to be dealt with (or carefully avoided) in order to secure acceptance through the ratification process. Thus, when the Declaration of Independence is referred to by courts, it is usually cited to establish the rationale behind Constitutional provisions, as in the following example: "Indeed, the guarantees [of judicial life tenure and no reduction of judicial compensation] eventually included in Art. III were clearly foreshadowed in the Declaration of Independence, which among the injuries and usurpations recited against the King of Great Britain declared that he had 'made judges dependent on his will alone, for the tenure of their offices, and the amount and payment of their salaries.'"[1] Similarly, the principles enunciated in the Declaration underlay the Thirteenth, Fourteenth, and Fifteenth Amendments to the Constitution and were cited in the civil rights debates in the Congress following the Civil War.[2] On the frontispiece of the pocket-size edition of the Constitution published by the Foundation for the United States Constitution is the following inscription: "The Declaration of Independence was the promise; the Constitution was the fulfillment."

Nevertheless, to say that the Constitution embodies

operational specifics effectuating the government structure to be established is somewhat misleading because the specifics are not, in many respects, very specific.[3] A comparison with other comparable documents of basic law highlights this fact. If one compares the length of the United States Constitution with those of other political entities influenced by it, the relative brevity of the U.S. Constitution is striking. The United States Constitution does not contain detailed proposals for governmental operation and limitation found particularly in constitutions written in the twentieth century. (While some state constitutions, such as Indiana and Vermont, follow the spare federal model, most are far more detailed. A compilation of federal and state constitutions prepared for the 1938 New York State Constitutional Convention shows that the federal constitution occupies eleven pages and that of Vermont is twelve pages long, compared to California's ninety-six pages and Alabama's fifty-three pages.[4] The New York Constitution, lengthy and detailed, includes, for example, a provision regulating the width of ski trails in the "forever wild" Adirondack State Park.[5])

Many have argued that, because the Constitution is primarily a statement of government structure and limitations on government, the glory of the Constitution is its flexibility, which allows growth and adaptation within the framework to meet the needs of differing times and circumstances.[6] On the other hand, this lack of specificity and flexibility makes it more difficult to evaluate a specific legislative proposal than it would be if there were a more lengthy detailed constitution that spoke directly to the constitutional issues raised by the proposal. To the extent that the Constitution does directly address the issue raised, it provides not only guidance for, but limits on, the legislator in his or her official role. But even a constitution with significant specificity cannot avoid all constitutional disputes.

Particularly in the description and limitation of rights, those who draft constitutions and constitutional amendments have found clarity and finality elusive.

Much of the discussion and debate at the Constitutional Convention related to the distribution of responsibility and power among the legislative, executive, and judicial branches of the government that was being created. Even more discussion and debate related to the distribution of responsibility and power between the states and the federal government then being created. The Constitution itself has virtually nothing to say on how and by whom conflicts between legislative acts (whether state or federal) and the Constitution are to be resolved.

The second paragraph of Article VI of the Constitution (generally known as the "Supremacy Clause") provides, "This Constitution, and the Laws of the United States which shall be made in Pursuance thereof; and all Treaties made, or which shall be made, under the Authority of the United States, shall be the supreme Law of the Land; and the Judges in every State shall be bound thereby, any Thing in the Constitution or Laws of any State to the Contrary notwithstanding." The Supremacy Clause clearly and unequivocally establishes the supremacy of the Constitution and laws made in pursuance thereof. But an anomaly persists: The phrase "[laws] made in Pursuance thereof" implies that there will be laws passed by Congress that are not "in pursuance of" the Constitution and that are therefore not the law of the land. But neither that phrase nor anything else suggests, either explicitly or implicitly, by whom or how such a determination of constitutionality is to be made. The fact that the Supremacy Clause implicitly recognizes the possibility of unconstitutional Congressional acts, while starkly raising the issue of who determines that fact, does not necessarily resolve the issue of the role or responsibility of

Congress in that determination. The role of constitutional arbiter could have been expressly assigned to or assumed by any one or more of the three branches of government. But it was not. (Interestingly, while the Supremacy Clause also specifically binds state court judges to the federal Constitution, it fails to mention state legislators, governors, or other state officials. One could certainly argue from that omission that the constitutional framers recognized the central role of the courts in the determination of constitutionality of legislation.)

Article III grants and defines the power of the judicial branch. But that Article, too, gives little guidance regarding the relative roles of the legislature and the courts in determining the constitutionality of legislation. After vesting the judicial power in one supreme and an indefinite number of inferior courts, Section 2 defines this judicial power:

> The judicial Power shall extend to all Cases, in Law and Equity, arising under this Constitution, the Laws of the United States, and Treaties made, or that shall be made, under their authority;—to all cases involving Ambassadors, other public Ministers and Consuls;—to all cases of admiralty and maritime Jurisdiction;—to Controversies to which the United States shall be a Party;—to Controversies between two or more States; between a State and Citizens of another State;—between Citizens of different States.[7]

There is nothing in Section 2 about whether the federal courts have the power to define and resolve conflicts between legislation and the Constitution.

The resolution of conflicts between legislation and the Constitution could have been expressly granted to the federal courts and, ultimately, the Supreme Court. In the most simplified version of such a scheme, the courts would have been named the sole arbiter, and neither legislator nor executive, state or federal, would have any power or obligation to assess the constitutionality of legislation under the Constitution. As we shall see, a number of legislators believe or assert that such matters are indeed solely the bailiwick of the Supreme Court. Such a position provides an easy escape for legislators who, either because of political pressure or because of determination to enact a piece of legislation, wish to avoid issues of constitutionality and vote for a bill generally assumed to be unconstitutional under Supreme Court precedents.

The function of determining the constitutionality of federal legislation could have been granted to the president. The Constitution itself gives the president the power to veto any act of Congress, subject to override by a vote of two-thirds of each house.[8] However the veto power does not refer to constitutionality, referring instead to the president's "objections" to the bill. Presidents have vetoed bills for many reasons, some petty and some of great consequence; unconstitutionality is only one such reason.

The function of resolving conflicts between the U.S. Constitution and state and local legislation could have been given to state governors and municipal executives. However, such a delegation involves different factors than a delegation to the president. The president of the United States is elected to represent all of the people in the United States, regardless of their states of residence; he is the chief executive officer of the nation, representing and speaking for the national interest. A governor or mayor, on the other hand, is elected by and represents only the state or municipality of which he or she is the chief executive; it is difficult for him or her to represent interests beyond those of the particular electorate. The unique role of the president is exemplified in circumstances that involve a conflict between the interests or concerns of one or more states and the federal government, or between the interests of several of the states. In such an event, it is appropriate and often necessary for the president to step in to assert, vindicate, and enforce the federal interest. Abraham Lincoln's actions asserting the national concept of union at the outset of the Civil War by fighting against secession is an obvious example. Andrew Jackson's dispute with various states over their allegations of the right to nullify federal taxes within their state boundaries is yet another. A more recent example is Dwight Eisenhower's deployment of federal troops in Little Rock to counteract Arkansas Governor Faubus's resistance to federal court school desegregation orders.

Finally, the constitutional arbitration role could have been granted to Congress. There is an obvious distinction between members of Congress and state legislators. As previously noted, the problems raised by delegating this authority to governors apply equally—perhaps even more graphically—to state and local legislators. While state legislators take an oath to abide by the United States Constitution, they are part of a state's governmental structure and thus likely to have a greater loyalty to local interests than to more broadly oriented national interests. But even in Congress, whose members are elected from districts solely within single states but are part of the federal establishment, the concept of granting congressional acts an irrebuttable presumption of constitutionality has not won the day.

Before moving on, it should be noted that similar questions exist about who is to determine the constitutionality of legislation passed by a state legislature that is possibly in conflict with that state's constitution. At least one state, New York, initially went off on a different course. The New York Constitution of 1777, written a decade before the federal

Constitution, provided for a Council of Revision, composed of five members: the governor, the chancellor (a judicial officer), and the then three justices of the New York Supreme Court.[9] Legislation was considered by the council after passage but prior to effectiveness, to avoid "laws inconsistent with the spirit of this Constitution, or with the public good, [which] may be hastily and unavoidably passed." The council could return a bill to the legislature with written objections. Such a veto could be overridden by two-thirds vote of both houses. In effect, the council combined the executive veto and judicial review. The council was abolished by constitutional amendment effective December 31, 1822.

Constitutional review by state courts of the constitutionality of state statutes has not been as controversial as the same issue on the national scene. It appears to be generally accepted on a theoretical or policy level, although unhappiness may be expressed about specific decisions or lines of decisions. There are at least three reasons for this general acceptance. In part it is because, until recently, the most hotly contested issues have been decided under federal rather than state constitutional principles.[10] The fact that the highest state judicial tribunals have judicial selection procedures that are, for better or worse, more politically responsive than those of the federal judiciary is a second likely factor. The third is an aspect of state's rights; somehow invalidation of state legislation by a court that is part of the state government is less offensive to a state legislature and citizenry than invalidation by a federal entity.

In *Congress and the Constitution,* the late Professor Thomas C. Morgan posited two basic approaches to the issue of who is to determine the constitutionality of legislation.[11] (Morgan focused solely on Congress, but much of his analysis applies equally to state legislators and legislatures.) Morgan called the first approach the "judicial monopoly theory" and the second the "tripartite theory." The judicial monopoly theory—that the sole and ultimate power to declare the constitutionality or unconstitutionality of a law or governmental act resides in the courts—is based on the following propositions:

1. Policy and constitutionality are distinct subjects which can be separated and assigned to different organs of government.
2. Constitutionality is a matter for experts, using specialized procedures, who are structurally independent from the other organs of government.
3. Only the judiciary meets the requirements of proposition 2.
4. Policy formation, determined by the struggle of political and other forces, is what legislatures and executives exist to do.
5. The legislature provides the arena for this struggle.
6. Accordingly, constitutional questions arising in Congress (or any other legislature) ought properly to be referred to the courts, unless the answers are clear. (How Morgan's exception for clear cases works is not obvious. What is a clear case to one observer is often not clear to another. And in the area of constitutionality, it is often the case that both the proponent and the opponent contend that their respective but diametrically opposite positions are clear and convincing.)
7. This arrangement is salutary because it provides a single, final umpire for all constitutional controversies and a representative body for policy.[12]

The tripartite theory—that, at least initially, each of the three coordinate branches of government can determine the constitutionality of its own acts—is stated by Morgan to be based on the following propositions:

1. The distinction between policy and constitutionality is illusory.
2. The Constitution makes no such distinction. Congress passes laws, not policy, and its members take an oath which requires them to inquire into related constitutional issues.
3. The Supreme Court has often given substantial weight to constitutional determinations in Congress. This must be based on an understanding and expectation that Congress will deal conscientiously with constitutional issues.
4. Constitutional questions are often more than merely technical. One component is community needs, attitudes and sentiments, which legislatures are better fitted than the courts to interpret.
5. Sole reliance on court determination may present difficulties, such as delay and public attacks on the courts when popular laws are invalidated.
6. Some constitutional issues never reach the courts for a variety of reasons. Thus, such issues will not be resolved, and may become an irritant in the polity.[13]

One can quarrel with some of the propositions set forth by Morgan as justifying one or other branch of government to act. For example, even if policy and constitutional issues are distinct subjects, sometimes pulling in opposite directions, this in my view has no relevance to whether legislatures should have a role or responsibility in the determination of constitutionality. Further, if legislatures are to have such a role, the question remains of what the role should be. Moreover, the fact that the "experts" in the judicial branch may as a practical matter have the final say in most instances[14] does not necessarily preclude the legislature from having a significant role in some instances and a preliminary screening role in all instances.

If a legislator has a responsibility to consider or determine constitutionality, Morgan's analysis also leaves open the question of how the legislator is to perform this responsibility and how can the legislator best assume the responsibility. For example, if the legislator has such a responsibility, does it mean that he or she is to attempt to ascertain what the Supreme Court would do if the case were to come before the Court, or does it mean that the legislator is to determine constitutionality independently of precedent or likely court rulings?

An analysis different from Morgan's has been put forward by Jesse Choper.[15] He assigns the respective responsibilities of the branches of the federal government based on the constitutional provision at issue. Dividing the major provisions of the Constitution into three general categories—those protecting personal liberties, those concerning separation of powers, and those allocating power between the national government and the states, Choper argues that the Supreme Court should generally abstain from exercising its judicial review function in the latter two categories, which, in his opinion, can best be resolved in the political and practical arenas. Only where constitutionally protected personal liberties are threatened should the Court intercede; personal liberties cannot be protected by the political process since the constitutional provisions were meant to provide protection against the "tyranny of the majority." (Choper truly gets to the crux of the issue, for public indignation at Supreme Court decisions is greatest regarding those issues where there is a clash between personal liberties and majority views, such as the abortion, school prayer, flag burning, and search and seizure cases.)

The period between 1789 and the 1803 decision of the Supreme Court in *Marbury v. Madison*[16] saw a variety of views on the role of the Constitution and the appropriate role of the Supreme Court in its interpretation. Thomas Jefferson saw the Constitution as an expression of the people, to be interpreted by the representatives of the people in Congress assembled.[17] Others have directed attention to Alexander Hamilton's Federalist, 78 which, in the course of arguing for life tenure for federal judges, referred to the judges as the people's representatives:

> No legislative act . . . contrary to the Constitution can be valid. . . . If it be said that the legislative body are themselves the constitutional judges of their own powers and that the construction they put upon them is conclusive upon the other departments it may be answered that this cannot be the natural presumption where it is not to be collected from any particular provisions in the Constitution. It is not otherwise to be supposed that the Constitution could intend to enable the representatives of the people to substitute their will to that of their constituents. It is far more rational to suppose that the courts were designed to be an intermediate body between the people and the legislature in order, among other things, to keep the latter within the limits assigned to their authority.[18]

This rather strange argument—that the people are better represented by federal judges who are not subject to election or recall by the people than by representatives who are—may well reflect Hamilton's more patrician inclinations. Some two hundred years later, the directly opposite view was expressed by Representative (later president) Gerald Ford during the debate on the proposed reversal by statute of the *Miranda* rule:

> I refuse to concede . . . that the elected representatives of the American people cannot be the winner in a con-

frontation with the U.S. Supreme Court. To admit that is to admit that the American people cannot control the U.S. Supreme Court.[19]

Jefferson, the primary draftsman of the Declaration of Independence and generally regarded as a leading proponent of the tripartite theory, eschewed granting the judiciary a monopoly in constitutional interpretation. In 1798, in response to the threat of war with France, spurred by Federalist leaders, Congress passed the Alien and Sedition Acts. While three of the Acts dealt with aliens, the Sedition Act focused on "domestic traitors." The Sedition Act criminalized the publication of "any false, scandalous or malicious writing . . . against the Government of the United States, or either House of the Congress, with intent to defame . . . or to bring them . . . into contempt or disrepute."[20] There was considerable concern, most notably among Democrat-Republicans, such as Jefferson, but also including the Federalist John Marshall, that the Sedition Act was unconstitutional. From a twentieth-century perspective, there seems little doubt that such a law today would be held to infringe upon First Amendment rights. It was, however, consistently upheld by the (Federalist) Supreme Court justices while they were sitting as trial judges on circuit, possibly a reflection of "war fever."[21] Its constitutionality never came before the Supreme Court sitting in that capacity (an example of the type of case Morgan referred to in his sixth proposition supporting the tripartite theory).

The Sedition Act expired by its terms on the day that Jefferson became president, and it was not renewed or extended. Jefferson ordered that all pending prosecutions be halted; he also pardoned all those previously convicted under the Sedition Act on the ground that the Act was unconstitutional. His approach is probably best expressed in a paragraph that appears in an early draft of his first State of the Union Message:

> Our country has thought proper to distribute the powers of it's [sic] government among three equal & independent authorities, constituting each a check on one or both of the others, in all attempts to impair it's constitution. To make each an effectual check, it must have a right in cases which arise within the line of it's proper functions, where, equally with the others, it acts in the last resort & without appeal to decide on the validity of an act according to its own judgment, & uncontrolled by the opinion of any other department. We have accordingly, in more than one instance, seen the opinions of different departments in opposition to each other, and no ill ensue.[22]

John Marshall's opinion in *Marbury v. Madison* in 1803 was the foundation stone for judicial review in the United States. As early as 1783, Marshall, like Jefferson a Virginian, led the Virginia Council of State, an executive governmental organ, in declaring unconstitutional under the Virginia Constitution a law giving the council the authority to investigate judges. In Marshall's words: "The [Council] are of opinion that the Law authorizing the Executive to enquire into the Conduct of a Magistrate . . . is repugnant to the Act of Government, contrary to the fundamental principles of our constitution, and direct[ly] opposite to the tenor of our Laws."[23]

Subsequently, in 1803 as Chief Justice of the Supreme Court, Marshall wrote the opinion of a unanimous court in *Marbury v. Madison*,[24] which has been viewed by some as the counterbalance to the tripartite theory and, in the words of Professor Leonard Levy, has achieved "mythic status as the foremost precedent for judicial review" of congressional acts for constitutionality.[25] The case arose when Jefferson, on taking office, refused to deliver the commissions of Marbury and certain other justices of the peace appointed at the very end of the Adams administration. Their nominations had been confirmed by the Senate. Curiously enough, their commissions had been signed by Marshall in his capacity as secretary of state in the Adams administration, but Marshall had failed to have the commissions delivered to the appointees prior to the change of administration.

Marbury brought a trial action directly to the Supreme Court, which issued an order to show cause directed to Madison, who had been appointed secretary of state. After a hearing, Marshall issued the opinion of the Court. Although he excoriated the Jefferson administration for failing to deliver the commissions to Marbury and his colleagues, Marshall held that the law that permitted Marbury to bring the action directly to the Supreme Court was in conflict with the Constitution and therefore void. Thus, Marbury's suit failed.

The decision was a politically clever victory for Marshall and the Court. The opinion attacked the Jefferson administration on the merits but did not require an order to Madison to deliver the commissions, an order that might well have been disregarded. At the same time, the Supreme Court established its right and duty to review congressional acts for compliance with the Constitution when the issue came before it in the context of litigated cases and controversies. "[A]n act of the legislature, repugnant to the Constitution, is void," because "the Constitution controls any legislative act repugnant to it." It is the appropriate role of courts to determine whether there is a conflict between the Constitution and a statute. "This is the essence of judicial duty."[26]

The decision in *Marbury* established the power of the Supreme Court to declare unconstitutional acts of other branches of the national government. It would seem logical that, if the Supreme Court had this power over coordinate federal branches, it would certainly have the power of judicial review over actions of a state. A few years after the *Marbury* decision, the Supreme Court established that aspect of its power as well.[27]

Once the Supreme Court held that the Court had the power to review and, if appropriate, invalidate congressional action as inconsistent with the Constitution, focus on the legal responsibility of the other two branches of the federal government was required. While *Marbury* firmly established the concept of judicial review and the role of the courts, the case did not negate the obligation or role of the other branches of government to act constitutionally and to make the provisional good faith determinations that enable them to do so. In particular, *Marbury* did not clearly establish that the courts had the exclusive right to resolve constitutional conflicts.

In 1822 Andrew Jackson vetoed a bill that would have rechartered the Bank of the United States because of his belief that it was unconstitutional. Responding to the argument that the bill was constitutional because that issue had been previously settled by decision of the Supreme Court, Jackson stated his reasoning as follows:

> The Congress, the Executive, and the Court must each for itself be guided by its own opinion of the Constitution. Each public officer who takes an oath to support the Constitution swears that he will support it as he understands it, and not as it is understood by others. It is as much the duty of the House of Representatives, of the Senate, and of the President to decide upon the constitutionality of any bill or resolution which may be presented to them for passage or approval as it is of

the supreme judges when it may be brought before them for judicial decision. The opinion of the judges has no more authority over Congress than the opinion of the Congress has over the judges, and on that point the President is independent of both. The authority of the Supreme Court must not, therefore, be permitted to control the Congress or the Executive when acting in their legislative capacity, but to have only such influence as the force of their reasoning may deserve.[28]

This is a remarkably strong statement of the most extreme tripartite view, since it seems to say that each of the branches operates independently of, and with no responsibility to, any other branch of government. Although Jefferson, in an early draft of his State of the Union speech, had written that he saw "no ill ensue" when different departments could reach opposing positions, it should be noted that both Jefferson's and Jackson's statements were made in the context of executive vetoes. The Constitution is not harmed when a bill is vetoed in an excess of constitutional caution, even though as a result the polity may be deprived of a worthwhile piece of legislation. Were the situation reversed—the Supreme Court finds an Act to be unconstitutional and the president signs an identical bill because of his contrary view—substantial constitutional mischief could result. This is not dissimilar to the situation that faced Richard Nixon after the Supreme Court denied his claim of executive privilege in withholding recordings of conversations in the White House. The only difference is that the Nixon choice dealt with executive action or inaction, rather than legislative enactment. Had Nixon adopted the Jacksonian view that the judges have no more authority over the president than the president has over them, an even greater constitutional crisis would have resulted.

Lincoln, too, struggled with the issue of the scope and manner of judicial review. In his First Inaugural Address he suggested that the Supreme Court ought not decide constitutional issues in the course of litigation coming before it,[29] though at other times he stated that Supreme Court decisions "should control" on Constitutional questions.[30]

The *Marbury* decision did not define the breadth of the binding impact of a Supreme Court decision. Some commentators, unhappy with the power of the Supreme Court under *Marbury*, have argued that what is binding on the other two branches is not the constitutional interpretation that underlies a decision of the Supreme Court, but rather the more limited decision that a particular action or statute conflicts with the Constitution and therefore must be invalidated. Therefore such persons would permit, or possibly even encourage, the executive or legislator to enact different legislation, if considered advisable, even though it would be unconstitutional if one accepted the Supreme Court's constitutional interpretation underlying the prior decision.

In 1958 the Court decided *Cooper v. Aaron*, which arose from the decision to send the Army to Little Rock to assist in the desegregation of a high school.[31] Arkansas contended that it did not have to comply with *Brown v. Board of Education* (the school desegregation case) because the Supreme Court decision was an unconstitutional assumption of power and, further, because Arkansas had not been party to the case. In response to those arguments, the Court expanded the far more discrete holding of the *Marbury* decision, stating "that the federal judiciary is supreme in the exposition of the law of the Constitution, and that principle has ever been respected by the Court and the Country as a permanent and indispensable feature of our constitutional system."[32] Thus both the Constitution and the decisions of the Supreme Court interpreting the Constitution were the supreme law of the land.

Attorney General Edwin Meese, in a speech given in 1987 at Tulane, attacked this assertion, arguing that a decision of the Supreme Court bound only the parties in the case; it "does not establish a supreme law of the land that is binding on all persons and parts of the government henceforth and forever more."[33] In one sense, Meese is correct. The order of the Court in a given case is directed to and is binding on the parties in the case. But in a broader and more important sense, he is wrong. Having correctly determined that the courts are to be the ultimate arbiter of the meaning of the Constitution, it would be an anarchic and wasteful system if the federal, state and local governments could simply disregard the existing judicial constitutional precedents as applied to those not a party to the original lawsuit or to a different factual situation. *Brown v. Board of Education* certainly had application to more than the Topeka, Kansas, school board. And while some municipalities and states continued to pass laws maintaining school segregation, such actions were correctly considered unlawful and perhaps even lawless. As Professor Burt Neuborne has so well put it, "constitutional law does not consist of an objective set of rules waiting to be discovered, but of the complex institutional interplay between an ambiguous text and the institution vested with the responsibility to declare its meaning."[34] To have the possibility of multiple authorized interpreters of the constitutional text with differing answers would be corrosive of the unifying role of a charter document, would prevent intelligent guidance for law-based action, and would cause the result of an act to differ depending on the forum in which it is considered.

A more difficult issue is raised when a legislator's deeply

held moral view is in conflict with constitutional precedent. During the Lincoln-Douglas debates, Lincoln said, "If I were in Congress, and a vote should come up on a question whether slavery should be prohibited in a new territory, in spite of that Dred Scott decision [holding such a prohibition unconstitutional], I would vote that it should [be prohibited]."[35] Similar conflicts arise today, usually with regard to issues affected by personal religious beliefs, such as prayer in the schools and abortion. As we shall see in the following chapters, Congress and state legislators pass laws that do in fact attempt to bypass or modify the established constitutional Supreme Court rulings. It is even more troublesome when, as we shall also see, the legislature uses the fact of the supremacy of the Supreme Court as an excuse to shirk its obligation not to pass unconstitutional legislation recklessly.

2

Children, Fear, and the Internet

Technological change usually causes fear and uncertainty. In the twentieth century, technological change has repeatedly revolutionized entertainment media and communications, as well as the storage, retrieval, and distribution of information. Each of these technological advances has brought with it the fear that the new technology would corrupt the young. First, motion pictures were decried as a corrupting influence, particularly with respect to sex. Help was sought from the government, since the state traditionally protects from deleterious influences those, like children, who are unable or less able to protect themselves. Censorship boards were created, only to run afoul of the First Amendment.[1] Ultimately, to mitigate the public outcry against the availability to minors of movies communicating "immoral" messages and information concerning sex, violence, and the like, the motion picture industry established its own rating system.

Motion pictures were originally only shown in movie theaters, and the theater owner or operator provided a focus through which regulation and control could be imposed. The introduction of VCRs and the resulting proliferation of video rental stores resulted in laws regulating display to minors of inappropriate material in such stores, as well as zoning laws that reflected an attempt to force stores carrying predominately "adult" materials to locate far from neighborhoods likely to be frequented by youngsters. Zoning and display laws are not as effective in controlling motion picture content as regulation of the theaters had been.

Many parents have viewed television from its inception as a greater threat than movies, since it brings entertainment, pictures, and information directly into the home. With the increase of one-parent homes and the increasing number of mothers employed outside the home even when not required to do so by economic circumstances, the "traditional" home setting of the ever-present mother able to guide or control the use of the home television set by children is not realistic, even in the prototypical middle-class family.[2] This has resulted in pressure on the government for V-chips and more informative rating systems.

When television first appeared on the scene, a family most likely had a single television set, generally in the living room, visible by and to all, and thus subject to control. Even as the price of sets decreased and the accessibility of television sets thus increased, some level of control, whether direct governmental control or less formal political pressures, could be imposed on the networks and the FCC license-holders. These controls, too, have become less effective with the dilution of the power of the major over-the-air networks by cable networks and independent stations.

Late in the twentieth century, the Internet became the pervasive new technology, available in public libraries to those who do not have the means or the inclination to purchase the requisite hardware. Remarkably, the Internet, in a period of approximately ten years, has grown from a system known only to a select few computer enthusiasts to a medium used by over 140,000,000 persons. Young people's ready access to the Internet has raised parental concerns to new heights. The blame addressed to the Internet after the 1999 Littleton, Colorado, school shootings because of the availability of bomb-making and death-oriented materials is an example of such concern. Nothing has appeared quite so uncontrollable, and thus threatening, to parents, as the Internet. To a great extent, the threatening aspects of the Internet are the flipside of its strengths. Information arrives from millions of sources throughout the world without any necessary intermediary (although, in many cases, the major service providers such as America Online have to a certain extent taken over the intermediary role). The Internet is interactive, so that a young person can converse with people throughout the world unknown to, and thus uncontrolled by, the parent. It is not a fixed medium like books, motion pictures, or pretaped television; thus it is not susceptible to prior review. Finally, as children get their own computers or ready access to school and library computers linked to the outside world, it is a medium that a child can use to receive information and communicate from the privacy or his or her own room without the knowledge or control of parents. While reading forbidden books after hours required at least a flashlight or dim light, which could be observed, the laptop provides a light source not easily detectable. It should thus be no surprise that pressure has developed for the creation of some appropriate governmental mechanism to protect children from harms asserted to be inherent in this new medium.

The pressure has been intensified by the commonly held belief that pornography is rampant on the Internet. Thus, with the Internet, as with motion pictures and television, sexual information and depictions of sexual acts were viewed as the primary threatened harm.[3]

Throughout history, a species of elitism has been one of the propelling factors behind censorship. As long as materials are limited to the elite, whether it be the educated, the well-to-do, or the politically powerful, there is little pressure for governmental censorship. If such materials become generally available, either because of diminished costs or advances in communications technology, or both, a need for censorship is perceived. The fact that censorship as a means of attacking the "danger" is often presented in a way that develops strong political support among the common persons whom it "protects" does not change this fact. In earlier times, dime novels, cheap theaters, and the like raised similar moral issues. In the 1930s, 1940s, and 1950s, the inexpensive and broadly distributed paperback book raised issues that had troubled no one when similar books were available only in more expensive hardcover versions. When, in the words of the Reverend James Pickett Wesberry, chairman of the Georgia Literature Committee, "a few public-spirited citizens at last became alarmed" at the "display of salacious material freely accessible to the young and impressionable at prices easily accommodated by young allowances, . . . [they] began to act [i.e., censor]."[4] In this context the Internet is an unusually democratic medium. Access is easy and broad. One can "publish" and broadly disseminate one's views at minimal cost without having to seek an intermediary publisher or broadcaster and, if one desires, can do so anonymously or pseudonymously. And anyone who signs on to the Internet has access to a broad panoply of information, views, and art.

The problem, however, is that governmental regulation

of depictions or descriptions of sexual conduct on the Internet within the constraints of the First Amendment is very difficult, because of the very facts that are the strengths of the medium. For First Amendment purposes, sexually explicit or frank material falls into one of four categories:

1. Material that is obscene and has no protection under the First Amendment. This is written or pictorial material which, taken as a whole, appeals to the prurient interest in sex, describes or depicts specified sex acts in a manner considered patently offensive under contemporary community standards, and has no serious value. It may be banned and criminalized wherever and however it appears.[5]
2. Material that is not obscene for the population generally but is deemed harmful to minors and therefore obscene in relation to that group. This is material that, taken as a whole, appeals to minors' prurient interest in sex, describes or depicts specified sex acts in a manner considered by adults to be patently offensive for minors under contemporary community standards, and has no serious value to minors. Basically, this is the general standard of obscenity modified to reflect the lesser maturity of a minor. The sale of such material to minors, or permitting minors access to the materials, can be prohibited, provided that such a prohibition does not at the same time prevent access by adults, for whom the material is constitutionally protected.[6]
3. Child pornography. This is material that visually depicts children engaged in sexual conduct or nude in a lascivious manner.[7] Since the underlying basis for the unique and separate categorization of child pornography is the need to protect children from abuse in the course of the creation of the child pornography, one need not consider

the material as a whole; nor is there a simple defense based on serious value of the material.
4. Indecent but constitutionally protected material. This category is vague and much harder to define. This material can be regulated in some situations, generally because of the way it is made available. For example, because radio and broadcast television make use of a governmentally regulated scarce resource (the airwaves) and because broadcasts enter the home without any affirmative choice by the recipient, the Supreme Court has held that reasonable regulation of indecent, constitutionally protected speech on radio and television broadcasts is permissible. The leading case upheld FCC penalties based on a monologue by George Carlin, including the "seven dirty words," which was broadcast on Pacifica radio.[8] Similarly, indecent material thrust upon an unwilling and possibly offended viewer or hearer by posters or public loudspeakers might fall into this category.[9]

Since material that is included in the first and third categories—that which is obscene or child pornography—is not constitutionally protected in relation to anyone, adult or minor, the fact that such material can be found on the Internet raises no particular problem. It can be banned and penalized at will. (There may, of course, be problems in finding the culprit, particularly if foreign-based, but these are not much different than the problems facing postal inspectors seeking to prosecute those who mail obscene matter and child pornography.) However, those concerned by the availability of sexual material on the Internet desire to extend the level of regulation further. They seek to limit the access of children and teenagers not only to material that is harmful to minors (as defined in category 2), but also to material that is indecent. Given the nature of the Internet and the constitutional requirement that there not be an undue restriction on the ability of adults to obtain constitutionally protected material, this was a difficult and complex, if not impossible, task.

During the 1990s, efforts to censor material on the Internet and control the Internet's availability to minors played out in Congress and state legislatures. Part of the difficulty in analyzing the Internet from a First Amendment perspective is due to its complexity, uniqueness, rapid development, and the ever-changing multiplicity of its uses and roles. In some ways, it is, like the telephone system, a common carrier. For example, the service providers have argued that, like the telephone company, they should not have any responsibility for the substance of what they carry. Those seeking to regulate the service providers claim that they are like a bookstores, choosing what they carry. But the roles are constantly changing; as this is being written, even service providers and search engines that started in a relatively passive mode are finding it advisable for business reasons to offer content or direction to users, thus blurring the distinction between mere carriers and content-providers.

The Internet also is used in many different ways, each of which raise different issues. To list a few, there is simple one-to-one e-mail when the two participants may or may not know one another other than through the Internet; there is e-mail addressed to a list, some or all of whom may not be known to the sender; there are "chat rooms," where persons having a commonality of interest or a commonality of circumstance can conduct conversations on a real-time basis; and there is the World Wide Web, consisting of information posted on the Internet for anyone to procure and interact with. Some uses of the Internet are commercial; some uses are intended as a public service and information; other uses are meant to convey information or purely personal messages. I am sure that between the time that this is being written and the publication date, new and interesting uses and modes of use will have been developed.

I shall examine how three legislatures went about the task of attempting to control the flow of information on the Internet for the stated purpose of protecting minors: Congress's passage of the Communications Decency Act of 1996 (CDA); the New York legislature's passage in 1997 of its Internet indecency law; and, finally, the New Mexico legislature's passage of its Internet indecency law, enacted in 1998 after both the CDA and the New York statute had been held unconstitutional. The examples show that when the political benefits of passing an unconstitutional law are significant, many legislators will allow their obligation to comply with the U.S. Constitution to fall by the wayside. Further, when political benefit derives merely from the appearance of doing something, it matters little to the legislator whether the statute survives constitutional challenge or, even if it did, whether it works. It is particularly troubling that, despite the complexity, novelty, and rapidly changing aspects of the Internet and despite the legislative branch's traditional function as fact finder, none of the three legislatures held hearings on the complex technical and legal issues raised by the bills. Only after passage, when the three statutes were challenged on constitutional grounds did such examinations take place, and then they took place before judges rather than before legislators.

Communications Decency Act

One of the significant legislative issues in Congress in the mid-1990s was telecommunications deregulation and reform.[10] For the most part, this had little to do with the relationship of most individuals to the Internet. But, from the outset, the bills embodying reform measures for the telecommunications industry became the vehicle for the imposition of censorship of sexual matters on the Internet. On July 26, 1994, Senator Jim Exon, a Democrat from Nebraska, offered an amendment to the then-proposed Communications Act of 1994, which would, among other things, have "modernized" the indecency provisions in already existing communications law to apply to the Internet.[11] The regulatory provisions of the Exon proposal were broad, sweeping, and vague. The proposed amendment provided that anyone who makes, transmits, or otherwise makes available on any "telecommunications device" any comment, suggestion, or other communication that is obscene, lewd, lascivious, filthy or indecent, or anyone who knowingly makes, transmits, or makes available on a telecommunications device any indecent communication for commercial purposes to a person under eighteen years of age or to any other person without that person's consent, is guilty of a felony, with a penalty up to a fine of one hundred thousand dollars and two years in jail. By criminalizing a wide and vaguely defined range of constitutionally protected communications, the proposed amendment was, at best, of very doubtful constitutionality. Although no hearings were held, in August 1994 the amendment was adopted by the Senate Commerce Committee, the Senate committee considering the bill, by a vote of 18-2. This was of no lasting impact, since the Communications Act of 1994 failed to pass.

Undeterred, Senator Exon, together with Senator Slade Gorton, a Republican from Washington, reintroduced the proposal as a freestanding bill on February 1, 1995. They stated:

> [T]he information super-highway should not become a red light district. This legislation will keep that from happening and extend the standards of decency that have

protected telephone users to new telecommunications devices.

Once passed, our children and families will be better protected from those who would electronically cruise the digital world to engage children in inappropriate communications and introductions. The Decency Act will also clearly protect citizens from electronic stalking and protect the sanctuary of the home from uninvited indecencies.[12]

This statement focuses on stalking and the importuning of children; it is followed in the *Congressional Record* by a reprint of an article from the *Washington Post* entitled "Molesting Children by Computer." But the senators failed to note that the bill would also ban safe sex information, serious gynecological and other scientific discussions relating to health and reproductive issues, AIDS prevention information, sexually frank e-mails between adults or between a parent and his or her teenage child, and sexually frank literary passages. Most important, there is no mention by the senators of either constitutional or practical impediments to the proposal.

On March 23, 1995, less than eight weeks later, with no discussion on the record about these issues, the Senate Commerce Committee agreed by a voice vote to append Senator Exon's bill to the Telecommunications Competition and Deregulation Act, numbered S.652. On the same day the Commerce Committee favorably reported S.652 for consideration by the full Senate.

Senator Patrick J. Leahy, a Democrat from Vermont, was most vocal in opposition to the bill, contending that a study by the Justice Department was required to evaluate the impact of the proposal on individual rights, and on copyright, privacy, antiobscenity, and child pornography laws. Leahy was also interested in information about alternative, less intrusive protective measures. Days later Leahy proposed a bill to that effect and made a statement raising both the practical and constitutional issues about the Exon proposal.[13] He also suggested that a coalition of industry and civil rights groups be asked to recommend an approach to regulation. While this has a tinge of letting the fox into the henhouse, Leahy's suggestion was needed. The Exon proposal demonstrated that there was a serious lack of knowledge about how the Internet functioned. It was clear that, in order to fashion a workable constitutional proposal, technical advice and knowledge was necessary. Only then could Congress determine whether it was possible to fashion appropriate legislation to deal with the concerns of the public without infringing on First Amendment rights.

In early May of 1995, Senator Leahy received a letter from the Justice Department in response to an earlier letter he had sent to Attorney General Reno, seeking her views on the Exon bill.[14] The department raised concerns about the bill, finding that the Exon bill "would significantly thwart enforcement of existing laws regarding obscenity and child pornography, create several ways for distributors and packagers of obscenity and child pornography to avoid criminal liability, and threaten important First Amendment and privacy rights." The Department concluded by recommending a careful review of the proposal. The substance of the Justice Department's letter was described by Senators Leahy and Russell D. Feingold (a Democrat from Wisconsin), in a May 16, 1995, letter to their fellow senators.

In response, Senator Exon sent a letter to the Senators dated June 7, 1995, in which, for the first time, he publicly acknowledged the existence of constitutional issues in connection with his proposal. Attached to the letter was a revised version of the bill which, Exon stated, had been "carefully constructed to be consistent with the Constitution." The revision was described as "a carefully balanced response to the growing concerns about inappropriate uses of telecommunications technologies . . . [which] will clarify that the proposed legislation does not reach constitutionally protected speech between consenting adults."

During the next week, Senator Leahy contended that the passage of any statute should be deferred so that the Justice Department could conduct the in-depth legal and policy review it had recommended not only in the letter to Senator Leahy, but also in a letter to Senator Exon. At the same time, Exon was adjusting the language of the bill to meet some of the arguments raised, resulting in the Exon/Coats Amendment introduced on June 13, 1995. During this entire period of discussion, there were no hearings to collect information, to hear from experts on the Internet regarding its operation and capabilities, to find out how the bill would affect protected speech and communication, or to ascertain whether the perceived dangers could be countered by others means. Rather, there were extensive private discussions held with, and pressure imposed by, both the religious right-wing groups who were actively supporting the CDA, on the one hand, and a combination of liberal and media groups opposing the CDA, on the other. Both sides pressured the senators to support them. In response to pressure from the powerful and well-funded on-line service providers, a series of "good faith" exemptions or defenses was added to the bill, and consequently those organizations no longer opposed the bill and were eliminated as a counterweight to the conservative religious groups.

On June 14, 1995, the bill reached the Senate floor. The Exon/Coats amendment was adopted by a vote of 84 to 16. But, as the scene shifted to the House, there followed what appeared to be a reaction to the restrictiveness of the Exon/

Coats proposal. Speaker Gingrich (not noted as a First Amendment proponent) raised questions about the wisdom and constitutionality of the CDA. A version of the CDA had been introduced in the House in early 1995, but was never considered on the floor. Rather, on August 2, 1995, during debate on the Communications Act of 1995, provisions known as the Internet Freedom and Family Empowerment Act, were added to that Act by a vote of 420-4. This proposal, authored by Representative Christopher Cox, a Republican from California, and Representative Ron Wyden, a Democrat from Oregon, was an attempt to give Congress the opportunity "to trust the creative genius of American technology and the sound judgment of American families" rather than "to put the future of the exciting, vibrant Internet and other interactive media in the hands of bureaucrats and regulators."[15] The bill did not include the prohibitory provisions found in the CDA. Rather, it would, among other things, have encouraged online providers to filter content by relieving them of liability for doing so. Thus, as the end of the year approached, the Senate and House had passed differing telecommunications reform bills with radically different provisions dealing with the availability of indecent materials to minors on the Internet.

A conference committee was appointed, heavy lobbying ensued, and on February 2, 1996, both the House and Senate passed a version of the Telecommunications Competition Act of 1996, which basically adopted the more restrictive approach of the Senate proposal. The Act was signed into law by President Clinton the following week. One addition to the CDA was a provision for an expedited judicial review of challenges to the statute. The reviewing tribunal was to be a three-judge trial court composed of one federal appeals judge and two federal trial judges, with an appeal as of right directly to the Supreme Court. The reasoning behind this provision was that, because the CDA had a potentially vast impact and because the constitutional issues were significant, it was important to have any constitutional issue resolved quickly. Such an expedited procedure, which has recently come to be viewed as a palliative for the benefit of opponents of legislation of doubtful constitutionality, does not mitigate most of the problems caused by passage of unconstitutional laws; nor does it resolve issues quickly, except relative to the much longer period of usual litigation.

Congress was considering legislation to regulate a medium agreed by all to be a major new force in the world—possibly *the* major force in the immediate future. When legislating on this matter of great importance and significance, Congress failed in its responsibilities in two related areas, collection of information for appropriate fact-finding and consideration of constitutional issues. The most remarkable aspect of Congress's inadequate fulfillment of its legislative responsibility is the absence of any hearings. One would have hoped that, faced with a new and, for many of the congresspersons, an unknown or barely understood phenomenon, extensive hearings would have been held to discuss what the Internet was, how it worked, and how it could be regulated. But there were none.

Professor (later Oregon Supreme Court Justice) Hans A. Linde described the legislative process of discerning rational policy as requiring, at a minimum, three elements: "Some knowledge of present conditions; the identification of a preferred future, or a goal; and a belief that the proposed action will contribute to achieving the desired goal."[16] The first and third of these elements require factual determinations. The lack of fact-finding hearings negatively affected Congress's ability to consider intelligently the constitutional issues raised by the CDA. With only a superficial understanding of how computers and the Internet work, comparing regulation of the Internet with regulation of phone communications, television, or cable, as was done, had a facial appeal; a full understanding of the Internet makes it clear that the analogy is meaningless and inappropriate.

The factual review upon which Congress should have embarked was eventually conducted by the trial court in Philadelphia, when, as explained below, the challengers of the CDA wired the courtroom and devoted five days to expert testimony about the Internet. The testimony demonstrated the technological and economic inability of plaintiffs and other users of the Internet to comply with the CDA. (Similarly, in the challenge to the New York State Internet indecency law discussed later in this chapter, plaintiffs provided the court with expert testimony as to the operation of the Internet, in part to rebut the foolish and almost delusional argument of the state that there were intrastate Internet communications that could be regulated by the state without affecting interstate communications.) The failure of Congress to do its job had a number of harmful effects. First, it put on the books and into effect a law that couldn't work and that was unconstitutional. Consequently, once the courts struck down the CDA, there was no federal legislation on the issue of indecent material on the Internet and minors. Second, Congress's failure to hold hearings shifted the burden of initiating and paying for the fact-finding process to the private sector. Third, the failure deprived Congress of the opportunity, with appropriate knowledge, to craft a constitutional and effective law that would carry out the at least some of legislators' intent. Had substantive hearings been held on the Internet and on the factual and constitutional issues raised by regulation of the Internet, the collective wisdom of Congress would have had the opportunity to try to fashion legislation that sought to meet constitutional requirements. Absent such hearings, the proceedings took place in the proverbial darkness.

Pursuant to the accelerated review proceedings authorized in the CDA itself, three lawsuits were brought in short order. Two were brought in Philadelphia, the third in New York. The first challenge, filed in Philadelphia on the day the bill was signed, was brought by the American Civil Liberties Union and nineteen other parties against the attorney general. The plaintiffs included Planned Parenthood Federation of America, the National Writers Union, the Electronic Frontier Foundation, and the Safer Sex Page.[17] Within days, a second suit was brought, also in Philadelphia, by a group of plaintiffs led by the American Library Association, whose interests and concerns were to a certain extent different from the ACLU plaintiffs'.[18] The court combined the suits.

On the day the CDA was signed and the ACLU brought its action, Joe Shea, the editor-in-chief, publisher, and part-owner of the *American Reporter*, a newspaper distributed solely on the Internet, published an editorial criticizing the CDA and quoting George Carlin's "seven dirty words." Since these words had been found to be indecent by the Supreme Court in *FCC v. Pacifica*,[19] Shea's action presumably violated the CDA. He brought an action in the federal court in New York challenging the law's constitutionality.

Since the Philadelphia cases relied to a great extent on the impossibility and impracticability of compliance with the CDA, vast amounts of factual evidence had to be developed, much of it dealing with the workings of the Internet. This is precisely the sort of factual information that Congress had never tried to obtain. Plaintiffs submitted more than one hundred factual statements from more than sixty witnesses, experts, and Internet users. Extensive depositions were held and factual stipulations were negotiated, culminating in five days of oral testimony at the trial. The legislative fact-finding function had been moved to the courtroom, where it was carried out in an adversary context.

The *Shea* case in New York did not move with quite the same speed. In an attempt to limit unnecessary duplication of effort, the New York three-judge federal court directed the parties to enter into a range of stipulations regarding the current state of the technology, incorporating relevant portions of the record in the Philadelphia litigation. (This was aided by the fact that Justice Department attorneys represented defendant Janet Reno in both actions.)

On June 11, 1996, the Philadelphia federal three-judge court unanimously held the CDA unconstitutional under the First Amendment. It found that the law, as a practical matter, restricted a substantial amount of adult protected indecent speech, a restriction that was neither narrowly tailored nor outweighed by the interest of the government in protecting minors. Two of the three judges also found the provisions of the law unconstitutionally vague.[20] Six weeks later, on July 29, 1996, the New York federal court came to the same conclusion, finding the CDA to constitute an unconstitutional ban on indecent communication, both protected and unprotected.[21]

Thus, at the first level, all six federal judges (two from the courts of appeal and four from the district courts) found the CDA constitutionally infirm. The government appealed both cases, and within a year the Supreme Court unanimously affirmed both decisions.[22] All fifteen of the judges and justices to consider the CDA found the prohibition on display of indecent material to minors to be unconstitutional.

The passage of the CDA is a prime example of the impact of recklessly passed legislation. While there may have been a constitutional way of controlling or affecting minors' access to sexual material on the Internet, the statute as passed was based on a misunderstanding or lack of understanding of the technology underlying the Internet, resulting in part from Congress's total failure to collect information at hearings and make fact-finding based on the information. Thus the cost of challenging the CDA and establishing the facts necessary to the challenge shifted to the groups mounting the challenge, many of which were not-for-profit organizations. (More than $475,000 of the funding for the American Library plaintiffs' suit came from the American Library Association and its affiliated group, the Freedom to Read Foundation.) The legal fees and expenses for the American Library Association plaintiffs were more than $1,200,000, representing more than five thousand hours of attorney time. The number of hours of work by ALA counsel would have been greater, but the consolidation of the two Philadelphia cases allowed the work to be divided between the ALA and ACLU attorneys. The legal costs and expenses for the ACLU plaintiffs exceeded $396,000.

As a result of the Equal Access to Justice Act,[23] plaintiffs were in a position to seek reimbursement of their fees and some of their expenses from the federal government. The hurdles to reimbursement under the act are high, however. If the government has a reasonable belief for the facts alleged, a reasonable basis in law for the theories propounded, and a reasonable connection between those facts and that law, there is no reimbursement. In such cases, the government has the opportunity to test the constitutionality of what turns out to be an unconstitutional statute on the financial backs of the challengers. In addition, reimbursement for legal fees is at a below-market rate ($75 per hour until 1996 and $125 per hour thereafter) and is not available to businesses with over five hundred employees or with a net worth of over

$7,000,000, or to individuals with a net worth of over $2,000,000.

Another result of the reckless passage of the CDA was the reinforcement of the belief held by some, often on the right end of the political spectrum, that courts—and in particular the Supreme Court—are liberal activist bodies that regularly cancel legislation passed by the legislative representatives of the people. The courts are unfairly attacked when, as in the CDA case, what happened was the passage of legislation of, at best, doubtful constitutionality with Congress's knowledge and expectation that it would be tested in the courts, and that the courts would take the heat in the political debate. Indeed, Congress itself provided an accelerated and simplified procedure for the fully anticipated court review.

Finally, had the CDA not been enjoined shortly after passage, proprietors of Web sites and others participating in the Internet would have had to determine whether to risk criminal prosecution or alter their use of the Internet.

With invalidation of the CDA by the Supreme Court, the scene next shifted to the states. At the same time that Congress was considering the CDA, similar concerns were presented to the state legislatures that were subject to the same political pressures as had affected Congress. The states were undeterred in their handling of the issue by the events in Congress. While the CDA as passed did include a preemption clause, a provision preventing state legislation regulating sexual content on the Internet,[24] until late in the game it was not clear whether the CDA would be passed, what would be in it, and how broad the preemption clause would be. Prior to the passage of the CDA, at least two bills that ultimately became law were con-sidered and enacted: one in New York and one in Georgia.

New York Statute

In New York state, members of the state senate, led by Senator William R. Sears, a Republican from the upstate Utica area, had been pressing for a state law to deal with the transmission of indecent materials to children by computer. In 1995, a bill passed in the Republican-dominated senate but did not obtain the required approval from the assembly. In January 1996, final legislative passage occurred, the bill (numbered Senate 210-D) having achieved strong bipartisan cosponsorship in both houses. As the CDA experience also showed, this was not a topic that a legislator could easily be hesitant about. There had been no hearings and it had not obtained high enough visibility to raise significant constitutional objections from groups outside the legislature other than the New York Civil Liberties Union. That group wrote a letter to Governor Pataki after the legislature passed the bill, urging that "the unique aspects of the Internet render the bill constitutionally problematic."[25] A likely reason for the lack of attention by the electronic media, computer groups, civil rights organizations, and others concerned about First Amendment rights on the Internet was that they were focused on the struggles in Congress revolving around the CDA and its alternatives. For the same reason that it is a traditional battlefield tactic to force an opposing army to fight simultaneously on various fronts, interest groups are generally ill equipped, both financially and in terms of knowledgeable personnel, to deal with major issues on a number of legislative fronts at the same time, particularly when one of those fronts involves a major, highly contentious fight in Congress, with significant operational and financial consequences for participants in the dispute.

The bill passed by the legislature in January 1996 was neither signed nor vetoed by Governor Pataki, and it did not become law. Apparently because of the passage of the CDA by Congress on February 2, 1996, the Sears bill was withdrawn for modification in light of the CDA. The Senate Introducer's Memorandum in Support of the successor to the Sears bill, now numbered Senate 210-E, stated:

> Amendments were necessary for the bill to be consistent with the recently passed Federal Communications Decency Act and Constitutional requirements. The amendments limit the application of the bill to exclude those who merely provided the defendant access to their computer or computer network.

In the same document, the "justification" for the bill is described as follows:

> Law enforcement agencies around the nation are becoming increasingly alarmed at the growing use of computer networks and other communications by pedophiles. Several cases have come to light wherein a pedophile has traveled clear across the country to have sexual relations with a minor initially contacted and engaged through various computer networks. . . .
>
> The recently passed federal crime bill contains provisions to address at least part of this issue: interstate travel for the purpose of having sexual relations with a minor. However, even if such travel does not occur and actual physical contact is not made between the pedophile and victim, the minor is still being exploited. For an adult to represent himself as a minor and engage another minor—male or female—in sexually infused communication is wrong[,] and when accomplished over a computer network or other communications system it is long-distance, high-tech sexual abuse. This bill addresses the issue of these communications.

The memorandum is curious in a number of respects. Part of Senate Bill 210-E does in fact deal with using the computer to importune a minor to engage in sexual acts. The constitutionality of this provision was subsequently sustained by a state court in the context of a prosecution,[26] as it should have been. However, another provision of the bill, which was ultimately challenged and stricken, criminalized the dissemination to any minor of material deemed harmful to minors, which is not "high-tech sexual abuse" by pedophiles. Leaving aside definitional issues, the bill would have forced all content-providers on the Web to erase from their material everything not appropriate for minors, thus preventing persons eighteen or older from having access to such constitutionally protected material. Similarly, conversations in chat rooms and on bulletins would have to be cleansed. It is also interesting that the federal preemption provision of the CDA is not mentioned in the memorandum.

The amended Sears bill, Senate Bill 210-E, was passed by the New York legislature in June 1996. By that date, three highly publicized challenges, one of them in a federal court in New York, had been brought against the CDA, the federal government had agreed not to enforce the CDA pending the decision of the Philadelphia court on the motion for a preliminary injunction, and extensive evidence had been submitted in the challenges raising significant issues regarding the technical, practical, and constitutional impact of the CDA. None of this was publicly considered by either house of the New York legislature; nor is there anything to suggest that these issues were considered in conference. In fact, the letter from Senator Sears to Governor Pataki in support of Senate Bill 210-E sent on July 11, 1996 (one month to the day after the decision of the unanimous three-judge federal court in Philadelphia holding the CDA unconstitutional), is identical to the letter that he had sent to the governor six months earlier in support of the 210-D version of the bill except that, while the earlier letter said that the "bill is consistent with past legislation" in the field, the June letter says that the "bill is consistent with the Federal Communications Decency Act as well as with existing state law" in the field.[27] No mention is made of the June 11, 1996, federal court decision in *ACLU v. Reno*, the preemption provision in the CDA that precluded any state legislation in the area, or of any other constitutional issue.

The public record indicates that the only suggestions of constitutional infirmities in the Sears bill that came before the governor were the January letter submitted by the New York Civil Liberties Union with respect to 210-D and a July 16, 1996, letter from the Media Coalition, a trade association that defends the First Amendment rights of publishers, booksellers, librarians, periodical wholesalers and distributors, recording and video games producers, and recording and video retailers in the United States.[28] The Media Coalition letter raised the First Amendment issues, referred to the decision of the Philadelphia federal court, raised the technological issues, and pointed out the federal preemption provision in the CDA.

On September 4, 1996, Governor Pataki signed Senate Bill 210-E. The approval statement does not mention the federal court decision. The only references to the CDA and constitutionality are the following:

> Recognizing the seriousness of this problem, Congress enacted the Communications Decency Act of 1966 to prohibit the interstate transmission of obscene telecommunications. This bill addresses intrastate communications and is consistent with the federal statute.

* * * *

> A number of publishers, on-line service providers, and Internet service providers have expressed the concern

that this legislation will infringe on the first amendment rights of adults and "chill" the growth of technology-related businesses in New York.... The first amendment objections to the bill are not persuasive, largely because the bill does not purport to regulate the nature of communications between adults.[29]

Prior to the issuance of this memorandum by the governor in connection with his signing 210-E, both the Philadelphia and the New York federal three-judge courts had held the CDA unconstitutional on bases relevant to the constitutionality of 210-E. The failure of the governor's memorandum even to mention these decisions is inexplicable. The governor, like the state legislature, made no attempt to deal with the serious constitutional issues raised by the federal courts' finding that the CDA was unconstitutional.

Also puzzling is the statement by the governor to the effect that the purpose of 210-E was to address intrastate, and not interstate, communications. Neither the language of 210-E nor the Introducer's Memorandum suggest such a limitation or legislative intent. In fact, the example given by Governor Pataki in his memorandum of the type of case justifying endorsement of the bill—communications between an adult male in Seattle, Washington, and a thirteen-year-old girl in New York State, then followed by an attempt to meet her in New York—is clearly an interstate communication. One can only surmise that in balancing the political danger in vetoing the bill against the reality of the federal preemption clause in the CDA, the governor's office considered it advisable to sign the bill on the premise that it was different than the one that had actually been passed by the legislature.

Shortly after the law became effective, a group of affected parties, once again led by the ACLU and the American Library Association brought a lawsuit against the governor and the New York attorney general before Judge Loretta

Preska in the federal district court in New York to challenge the New York statute. The statute was challenged on two grounds: first, the violation of the First Amendment, an argument similar but not identical to the challenge to the CDA. The state statute restricted material on the Internet that was "harmful to minors," a somewhat more restrictive standard than that of "indecency" found in the CDA. Although the precise nature of the material was different, the question of whether and how adults would be affected remained the same. The second ground was that the state law violated the Commerce Clause of the United States Constitution, that the state regulation unduly interfered with commerce and communications between the states. This argument had not previously been raised because of the CDA preemption provision. Since the CDA had been preliminarily enjoined on the ground of unconstitutionality, the viability of its preemption clause was not clear. Even though the preemption clause had not been specifically challenged, if the three-judge panel's finding of the unconstitutionality of the CDA was upheld (as, in fact, it was), it was unclear whether the preemption clause could be enforced after the substantive federal regulation with which it was allied had been invalidated.

Once again, the federal court was faced with a statute passed without any legislative hearings to collect information or legislative fact-finding about the premises underlying the constitutional and factual arguments mustered in support of the statute. The state's major argument was that the statute was limited to regulation of intrastate communications. It also from time to time suggested that the statute was limited in other ways not readily apparent from the statute, as, for example, that it did not apply to Web pages.

The plaintiff organizations that were concerned about the expense of the litigation and the time needed to complete the proceedings, made various time- and cost-savings proposals prior to the trial-type hearing. The first and most sweeping was that the state agree not to enforce the statute pending the decision by the United States Supreme Court in *ACLU v. Reno*, the appeal from the Philadelphia case, so that issues that might be resolved in that case would not have to be relitigated. The suggestion was ultimately rejected by the state attorney general's office, which was representing the governor and attorney general. Although a number of reasons were given, it appeared that the reason was political. The same reasons that impelled the governor to sign the law without reference to six judges having held a similar federal law unconstitutional apparently prevented the governor and the attorney general from agreeing to a voluntary stay for the few months until the Supreme Court would decide the issues. Similarly a suggestion to stipulate to the facts found by the federal judges in the Philadelphia case was initially totally rejected, although a few stipulations were ultimately the subject of an agreement. As a result of the refusal to enter into stipulations, extensive depositions were taken, declarations were prepared and executed, and a three-day hearing was held for which the courtroom was "wired" so that experts could testify for the benefit of the court and the parties about both the technological impossibility of regulating intrastate transmissions while leaving interstate communications free of such regulation and the practical impossibility of restricting communications to minors while leaving communications to adults free from such regulation.

At these proceedings, the plaintiffs were represented by a coalition of paid and volunteer counsel. Acceptance by the state of either of these proposals obviously would not only have eased the monetary burden on plaintiffs but also would also have reduced the time required for plaintiffs and their counsel to prepare and litigate. The benefits of a stipulation would have run both ways. The attorney general's office has much to do and must prioritize its time just as plaintiffs' counsel must. Further, the case was brought under a federal civil rights provision that grants a successful plaintiff reimbursement of its reasonable fees and expenses.[30] Thus citizens have an interest both in having the attorneys for the state use their time in the most productive manner possible and in limiting the cost to the state of payments to successful plaintiffs in constitutional challenges.

On June 20, 1997, just prior to the decision of the Supreme Court in *ACLU v. Reno,* Judge Preska issued a decision granting a preliminary injunction based on a violation of the Commerce Clause.[31] The judge found that the Internet is wholly insensitive to geographic distinctions and that no aspect of the Internet can feasibly be closed off to users from another state. She concluded that the state statute could not be limited to purely intrastate communications because there are no such communications when communicating on the Internet.[32] Comparing the Internet to the nation's railroads, the judge found that possible inconsistencies in regulations imposed by the various states was intolerable. The court deferred its decision on the First Amendment challenge pending the decision by the Supreme Court.

After the Supreme Court decision invalidating the CDA, defendants agreed that the preliminary injunction could be converted to a permanent injunction and a declaration of unconstitutionality. Plaintiffs filed papers evidencing fees and expenses of over $600,000; after negotiations, the parties agreed to an order granting plaintiffs $460,000 reimbursement from the state for fees and expenses.

As poorly conceived as was the substance of the CDA passed by Congress, the passage by the New York legislature of 210-E was far more irresponsible. Not only had there had been no hearings and evidently no other fact-finding, but, by the time 210-E was before the legislature for final passage, three highly publicized suits had been brought challenging the CDA, on which the bill appears to have been modeled. In those cases extensive evidence had been presented that cast great doubt on the technological premises and constitutionality of 210-E. The harm was compounded by the governor when he signed the bill, for he disregarded both the language of 210-E and the decisions of the federal courts concerning the CDA. Finally, the effects of politics on the litigation, as shown by the conduct of the attorney general's office in defending the action, cost the state nearly half a million dollars and used many hours of the attorney general's staff time to no real purpose.

Before getting to the New Mexico story, it is appropriate to mention one other statute, to show the similarity of the issues that arose in connection with different efforts to regulate Internet content. At about the same time that the New York legislature considered and passed 210-E, the Georgia legislature passed a law prohibiting the anonymous or pseudonymous messages on the Internet. Called the Georgia Computer System Protection Act,[33] it also raised constitutional issues under both the First Amendment and the Commerce Clause. Enacted in April 1996, after the commencement of the suits challenging the CDA, it, too, was challenged by a group of plaintiffs led by the ACLU. The state's response, like that of the New York attorney general discussed above and, as we shall see, the New Mexico attorney general, was to argue that the statute really was something different than it seemed, requiring fraud or misappropriation of someone else's name, rather than simply a pseudonym. On the same day that Judge Preska declared 210-E unconstitutional, a federal district judge in Atlanta declared the Georgia statute violative of the First Amendment, dismissing the state's argument as not supported by the statute.[34]

New Mexico Statute

The next chapter in this saga took place in New Mexico. One would have thought that, after the Supreme Court decision in *ACLU v. Reno* and the federal district court decision in *ALA v. Pataki*, legislators would be cautious before venturing into the arena of Internet content regulation. Nevertheless, at the request of the New Mexico attorney general's office, State Senator Stuart Ingles, who acknowledged that he doesn't own a computer, late in 1997 proposed a bill that made it a felony to "lure" a minor for sexual purposes by means of a computer communication. This portion of the bill was similar to the part of the New York statute that was not challenged in *ALA v. Pataki* and that was subsequently upheld by a New York state trial court.[35] However, another portion of the bill, like the CDA and 210-E, prohibited the transmission to minors of "indecent" or "harmful to minors" material to minors. (The statute is unclear as to which standard applies. The heading refers to "harmful to minors"; the text refers to "indecency.") Even Senator Ingles had problems with this part of the law. A news report quotes him as believing that the on-line content provisions would be difficult to enforce on a state level and were secondary and not a large part of the debate surrounding the law. "I don't know how you would enforce the law."[36] With only token opposition, the bill soared through the New Mexico legislature in the final weeks of the session.[37]

To a certain extent, this appears to be an example of a legislator, and perhaps his colleagues as well, misled by the attorney general's staff, which pushed an unconstitutional statute. On the other hand, a senator was reported in the

Albuquerque *Journal* to have indicated that many of the legislators knew that the bill was probably unconstitutional when they voted for it.[38] After passage but prior to the governor's signing the bill, the proponent of the bill in the attorney general's office argued that it should, and presumably would, be read differently than the apparent plain meaning of the words, so that the statute would apply only to luring minors over the Internet. In any event, he stated, it was too late to modify the language so that the bill would say what the attorney general's office contended it meant, rather than what it actually said.[39] Despite a letter to the governor from the Media Coalition pointing out the relevant United States Supreme Court and New York federal district court decisions, Governor Gary Johnson signed the bill.[40]

Once again a lawsuit challenging the constitutionality of the statute was brought in the federal district court on April 22, 1998, by the ACLU and various trade association members of Media Coalition, such as booksellers, publishers, and librarians. After a two-day hearing in June 1998, during which the judge characterized the attorney general's reinterpretation of the statutory language as "mere sophistry," the court issued a preliminary injunction against enforcement of the statute relying on *ACLU v. Reno* and *ALA v. Pataki*, a decision that the state is appealing to the Court of Appeals. Once again it is likely that a state will pay for the legal fees of the mostly not-for-profit groups challenging an unconstitutional statute.

What can be learned from the New Mexico experience? One can be somewhat facetious and say that the lesson is not to pass legislation that is very similar to that which has previously been held unconstitutional, even if the state attorney general's office says that it means something other than what it appears to say and therefore is constitutional.

More seriously, this should have been a relatively easy call for a legislator. The U.S. Supreme Court had already said that a similar statute barring the transmission of indecent material provision could not pass the test of the First Amendment, and a federal district judge in New York had already said that a virtually identical statute could not pass the test of the Commerce Clause. What more did a legislator need?

The issue was complicated by the role of the attorney general's office. The office of the chief legal officer of the state was the initial moving force behind the bill and, to the end, argued its constitutionality, including arguing a meaning of the bill that distorted its plain language. Despite the influence of the attorney general's office, there appears to have been a general understanding among legislators that this was a bill that raised significant constitutional issues but did not address them.

Child Online Protection Act

From the time that the Supreme Court unanimously found the CDA to be unconstitutional, there were discussions in Congress about a successor to the CDA that might pass constitutional muster (often referred to as "CDA II"). As a result, slightly more than a year after the Supreme Court decision, Congress passed the Child Online Protection Act ("COLA"). Once again the stated goal was "to protect children from being exposed to harmful material found on the Internet."[41] In an attempt to meet the objections of the Supreme Court, COPA begins with congressional findings that it is currently "the most effective and least restrictive means by which to satisfy the compelling government interest,"[42] COPA is limited to material which is harmful (i.e., obscene) as to minors which is commercially distributed, and COPA is limited to the World Wide Web, leaving unregulated many chat rooms, bulletin boards, e-mail, and the like. (Since Web sites are becoming interactive and may include, for example, e-mail capability, this division is no longer as neat as Congress may have believed it to be.)

Once again there were no hearings. Congress did acknowledge its lack of the predicate knowledge by providing in COPA for the establishment of a Commission on Online Child Protection to conduct a one year study "regarding methods to help reduce access by minors to material that is harmful to minors on the Internet," including the various technological tools and devices.[43] Congress thus reversed what was the normal pattern; rather than fact-finding followed by legislation, COPA represents legislation that followed by fact-finding.

COPA was signed into law on October 21, 1998. The very next day a lawsuit was brought in the federal court in Philadelphia by the ACLU, the American Booksellers Foundation for Free Expression, Salon Magazine and others,[44] challenging COPA's constitutionality. On November 19, 1998, just before the date that the provisions of COPA would have become effective, the district judge issued a temporary restraining order preventing the law from becoming effective because the claims of unconstitutionality had substance and should be heard. After evidentiary hearings, a preliminary injunction against enforcement of COPA was issued on February 1, 1999, the court finding COPA to have many of the same First Amendment deficiencies as the CDA.[45] Yet again Congress had barged ahead with a regulation of Internet content of questionable constitutional status.

Conclusion

The treatment of the issue of children and indecent Internet transmissions is an example of irresponsible legislating in its purest form. At the outset there was an issue that generated citizen concern—shielding children from what many believe to be inappropriate Internet communications. As the problem became a political issue, many of the nuances of the issue, both factual and legal, disappeared. In an effort to reach a result politically acceptable to their constituents, legislators declined to examine the factors, both factual and legal, that would affect the constitutionality of the legislation. They failed to explain to their constituents that using the Internet to lure or induce unlawful sexual relations with a minor raises different issues than the transmission of frank sexual passages from literature or transmissions on the obgyn.net Web site that features physicians frankly responding to questions from women throughout the country. The former is almost universally acknowledged to be harmful and subject to restriction; in fact, many think that such actions are proscribed under laws already on the books. The latter is thought by most people to be valuable speech. In the legislative process, the question became oversimplified, since these important distinctions diminish the political benefit of a starkly black-and-white picture. In both New York and New Mexico, and to a certain extent in Georgia as well, the fear generated by the specter of child-luring through the Internet became the engine for the passage of far broader legislation. It is easier to say to the public that the Internet should be cleaned up than to say that, while the Constitution permits the criminalization of luring children through the Internet to participate in illegal and harmful sexual acts, the Constitution protects medical information, literature, and other sexual materials against regulation. Politics becomes the leveler.

Congressional conduct displayed another important aspect of public behavior. The CDA debate did not focus to the same extent as the state law debates on luring as the basis of Internet regulation. Rather the debate and discussion on the CDA was bifurcated, focusing both on the possibility or, as the proponents of the CDA saw it, the likelihood, that minors, while doing research for their school homework on the Internet, would inadvertently and unknowingly stumble into an explicit sexual Web site, and the desire to prevent teenagers in search of sexual information or stimulation from seeking out such sites. (A question regarding the extent to which these concerns of some legislators were genuine rather than merely politically based is raised by the treatment of the Report of Independent Counsel Kenneth Starr in September 1998. Many of the same congressional leaders who led the fight for the CDA spearheaded the decision for Congress to release the Starr Report, containing many graphic descriptions of explicit sex, directly on the Internet. Schoolchildren did not inadvertently stumble upon this material on the Web; they actively were directed to it by congressional announcements and publicity.)

In each of the Internet content regulation efforts, the political pressure from the religious right as part of its more general push to limit the availability of sexual images, information, and discussion in the society and the perceived political benefit of enacting legislation to protect children from indecent influences militated against a more thoughtful and nuanced approach. The lack of substantive hearings was politically beneficial to legislative proponents of regulation because their efforts were not hampered by consideration of the factual, technological, and legal complexities. Legitimate hearings that have as their genuine concern factfinding and issue-finding not only clarify the facts and opinions but also expose the opposing positions to the harsh light of debate and publicity. They thus enable creative resolutions of public concerns.

Finally, there simply appeared to be a lack of will to grapple with the constitutional issues. During consideration of the CDA, the senators (other than Leahy and Feingold) seemed unwilling to deal with the issue, forging ahead without modification of their initial plans. Even after the constitutional issues had been somewhat clarified, the New York statute was passed and signed. And even after the level of legal precedent included a decision by the United States Supreme Court, the New Mexico law was passed and was signed, refuting any assertion that the problem arose from the ambiguity or absence of Supreme Court precedent. Rather, in these instances, the political imperative overcame the constitutional obligation. As a result, the highly emotional and politicized issue of children's access to sexual material on the Internet was forwarded to the judiciary, which, in annulling the three statutes, appeared to thwart the actions of the people's representatives. It was not the courts but the people's representatives who failed not only the people but also the Constitution they had sworn to uphold.

3

The Wright Brothers' First Plane Didn't Fly Either

      A dedicated and well-credentialed author/sponsor of legislation of doubtful constitutionality, particularly when supported by politically influential groups, can have a major role in causing such legislation to be passed. In this chapter and the next I will examine two such examples.

      In 1983, Catharine MacKinnon, a law professor who had achieved renown for developing the concept of and the framework for treating sexual harassment in the workplace as a tort for which a remedy was available, and Andrea Dworkin, a feminist poet and writer, developed a proposed ordinance to control sexually oriented material. The proposal arose out of a class on pornography given by MacKinnon and Dworkin at the University of Minnesota Law School.[1] The ordinance was developed on a civil rights antidiscrimination model. Pornography was defined as "the sexually explicit subordination of women, graphically or in words." The proponents of the ordinance considered pornographic material as defined in the ordinance to be comparable to a weapon or action rather than speech because of the harm that the material allegedly caused women. Thus, they argued, the material could be regulated and restricted because it was not protected by the First Amendment. To afford greater specificity, the proposed ordinance listed nine examples of pornography, a list that was not intended to be exclusive:

1. women presented as sexual objects, things or commodities;
2. women presented as objects who enjoy pain or humiliation;
3. women presented as sexual objects who experience sexual pleasure in being raped;
4. women presented as sexual objects tied up or cut up or mutilated or bruised or physically hurt;
5. women presented in postures of sexual submission or sexual servility, including by inviting penetration;
6. women's body parts—including but not limited to vaginas, breasts, and buttocks—are exhibited, such that women are reduced to those parts;
7. women are presented as whores by nature;
8. women are being presented by objects or animals; and
9. women are presented in scenes of degradation, injury, torture, shown as filthy or inferior, bleeding, bruised, or hurt in a context that makes these conditions sexual.

The categories of pornography listed in the proposal (and others unlisted) were defined as discrimination against women and declared to be violations of the applicable civil rights laws. Under the proposed ordinance, various civil (i.e., noncriminal) and administrative remedies were available, and these included injunctions against sale or distribution of the offending material. The MacKinnon/Dworkin proposal formed the basis of an ordinance passed by the Minneapolis City Council in 1983, an ordinance passed by the Indianapolis City Council in 1984, and an ordinance enacted by initiative by the voters in Bellingham, Washington in 1988.

Pornography, as defined by the MacKinnon/Dworkin proposed ordinance, went far beyond the U.S. Supreme Court's definition of obscenity, that is, sexually explicit material that was outside of the protection of the First Amendment. Thus, the ordinance's constitutionality was, at best, doubtful. (There were also serious questions about the power and authority of the city to enact the ordinance.) The specifics of the First Amendment constitutional analysis are not necessary for the purposes of this discussion, although it should be noted that ultimately, after passage in Indianapolis, the ordinance was found unconstitutional by a federal trial court and the federal court of appeals, which decision was affirmed by the United States Supreme Court.[2] What is relevant is that two legislative bodies—the Minneapolis City Council and the Indianapolis City Council—enacted this legislation at a time when most First Amendment scholars believed it to be unconstitutional. In Minneapolis it was passed twice. And the people of Bellingham, Washington, passed the initiative years after the nearly identical Indianapolis ordinance had been held unconstitutional by the courts. The circumstances are worth examining for what we can learn about legislators and the legislative process that led to these passages.

Minneapolis, in the 1970s and early 1980s, was a community concerned about the proliferation of "adult" bookstores and shops, and about a perceived inability to deal with the problem in a way that would pass muster with rulings under both the state and federal constitutions. A zoning ordinance passed in 1977 to prevent such "adult" retail establishments near residential areas, churches, and schools was held unconstitutional in 1982.[3] As with indecency on the Internet, discussed in the preceding chapter, citizen concern, to some extent manipulated by political forces, provided the backdrop for a desire (some might say demand) for legislative action. At the same time, some community leaders began to focus on what they saw as the antiwoman aspects of pornography, particularly in its more violent genre.

It was happenstance that these concerns were percolating in Minneapolis at the same time that MacKinnon and Dworkin were at the major law school in the city giving a course that focused on the MacKinnon/Dworkin legislative proposal for control of gender-discrimination by using remedies not based on criminal sanctions but on injunctions, fines, and damages. From one point of view, it was a perfect bill—censorship was to protect civil rights rather than limit them. Politically, it would have broader support than most proposals for censorship of constitutionally protected material, because it appealed to "both feminists and conservative 'law and order' types."[4]

A zoning hearing was held in Minneapolis on October 18, 1983. Arrangements had been made for Dworkin and MacKinnon to be present. They forcefully presented their perspective and their proposed ordinance to the city council. As a result of the presentation and following discussions, Charlee Hoyt, a Republican council member who had supported Ronald Reagan yet was a feminist, agreed to sponsor the proposal; MacKinnon and Dworkin were hired as consultants to the city council to draft the proposal as an amendment to the Minneapolis civil rights ordinance. The draft was submitted to the council one month later, in November 1983.

The terms of the consulting agreement provided that

> The Consultants shall perform all necessary services under the direction of the City Attorney in regard to amending the Minneapolis Civil Rights Ordinance in order to define pornography as sex discrimination including but not limited to drafting an ordinance relating pornography to sex discrimination; developing testimony of experts and other knowledgeable individuals that would show how pornography adversely affects women and is part of women's socially subordinate status; and consultation with the City Attorney and the City Council regarding legal and social issues raised by the ordinance.[5]

Services under the agreement commenced November 8. 1983, three weeks after the testimony at the zoning hearing.

The scope of services to be provided by MacKinnon and Dworkin demonstrates how the legislative fact-finding function of the city council was skewed. The charge to MacKinnon and Dworkin was not to develop testimony on the subject of whether pornography adversely affects women; rather, the charge was to develop testimony that would show that it did, thus bolstering the underlying premise of their own proposal. As Assistant City Attorney David Gross, the city's leading obscenity prosecutor, pointed out,

> They [MacKinnon and Dworkin] wanted to establish the philosophy of the ordinance despite existing legal and constitutional doctrine in the state and despite the facts....
>
> [Was the process biased?] Sure. They called all the

witnesses they wanted at the hearings. . . . They talked to Al Hyatt [Gross's colleague, another assistant city attorney], but they didn't want him asking any questions—only Kitty [MacKinnon] could ask questions. And there was no cross-examination. Only anecdotal evidence was presented. . . .

In this case, the consultant, who was also the advocate, was paid by the council, the City of Minneapolis, to lobby the council. So you had the council lobbying itself, with scheduled hearings where all the time was taken up by the consultant advocate. I said to myself, "Well, you know what a stacked deck is. Well, that's a stacked deck!" So, factually, the council hired an advocate to consult with the City Attorney's Office. But in actuality, we were cut off. Comments by Al Hyatt and me [which dealt with free speech concerns and First Amendment case law] were essentially rejected out of hand. . . . And we raised the First Amendment questions very early on because they are so obvious.[6]

The failure to conduct substantive, open-minded fact-finding on the basis of which legislators can make sensible policy and constitutional decisions is a recurring theme in many of the examples discussed in this book. Sometimes no hearings are held, as occurred when various legislatures passed the Internet anti-indecency laws discussed in chapter 2. At other times, selected witnesses presenting only, or predominately, one position are called to testify, as in the hearings on the Omnibus Crime Control Act, which will be discussed in chapter 6. Basically, this is what happened in both Minneapolis and Indianapolis with respect to the MacKinnon/Dworkin proposal. Policy determination based on accurate fact-finding and consideration of competing interests is one of the strengths of the legislative process;

skewing the hearing process constitutes a significant weakening of a foundation of that process.

Much of the testimony and discussion concerning the amendment consisted of anecdotal tales of abuse, rape, and violence, all allegedly caused or encouraged by pornography as broadly defined in the amendment. Passage of the amendment was described as a watershed that would generally improve the status of women and highlight the extent of male domination in society. During much of the hearing, the chair permitted MacKinnon to present the witnesses and conduct the questioning. The testimony of those who opposed the amendment was received with hostility by the spectators at the hearings and by some of the members of the council. In addition, the amendment's rapid movement through the legislative process gave opponents only a limited opportunity to review and comment on the proposal. The emotional intensity of the hearings was increased by demonstrations and vigils held by proponents during the hearings and consideration of the amendment.

There was little discussion of possible unconstitutionality. While there had been a November 1983 letter to the city council from the city attorney's office questioning the constitutionality of the proposed ordinance, it appears not to have been disclosed to the full council. It came to light in an article in a Minneapolis newspaper in March of 1984, well after the ordinance had been passed.[7] Apparently, those pressing the ordinance were not interested in a full discussion of the issue of the bill's constitutionality.

The MacKinnon/Dworkin proposal was clearly on a fast track. Hearings on the amendment were held on December 12 and 13, 1983, it was unanimously approved by the Government Operations Committee on December 22, and it was adopted by the full council on December 30 by a one-vote margin (7-6). The mayor of Minneapolis, the library board and the city attorney's office (with whom MacKinnon was ostensibly consulting) all urged a delay to consider the amendment's constitutionality.[8] Their pleas were joined by the Minneapolis Civil Rights Office, the very agency that was to enforce the ordinance if it passed. Nevertheless, the adoptive process inexorably moved on. Some of the haste may be attributed to the fact that the terms of office of five of the council members would end on December 31, 1983. Of these five, three voted in favor of the amendment and two voted against, providing the one vote margin for passage.

After passage, the amendment went to Don Fraser, a liberal who was the mayor of Minneapolis. National and local groups on both sides of the issue wrote to the mayor, urging veto or approval. On January 5, 1984, Mayor Fraser vetoed the amendment as unconstitutional. He also found that the city had no power to enact the provisions of the bill that created new grounds for civil rights claims between parties who have no relationship to the city. Fraser went out of his way to compliment the proponents of the amendment for their "skillful analysis of an issue rarely discussed in the public policy arena" and "applaud[ed] their leadership for social change." The tone of the veto letter clearly reflected the political support that had developed for the concepts that underlay the bill. At the same time, Fraser decried the fact that the city council had failed to heed the request that he, together with the library board and the Civil Rights Commission, had previously made for a more considered, less hasty, examination of the proposal:

> The City Attorney has had no opportunity to provide either a detailed legal analysis of the ordinance or to render an opinion on its constitutionality. My conversations with several staff members from the City Attorney's office indicate that they have raised and

are researching serious questions about the ordinance. They should be given the time to provide their opinion. Affected agencies should be given time to review and comment on that opinion. More work must be done before deciding whether or not such an ordinance should become part of our city's laws.

Fraser suggested that the Council refer the bill back to committee until the city attorney's review was completed. The mayor also indicated that he would be willing to consider "a more carefully drafted document."

The veto letter highlights a number of relevant issues. The mayor emphasized the deliberative aspect of the legislative process. He made the important point that fair examination of proposed legislation requires sufficient time to assure that legal issues can be explored. Such an examination is particularly significant when a new approach is being considered and when the country's basic document is involved. Further, the mayor understood the importance of having the opinions of legal counsel and of the affected agencies, although he does not say what weight should be given to the their views.

The story does not end with the mayor's veto. A few days after the veto, Laurence Tribe of the Harvard Law School, a leading constitutional scholar, joined the debate by sending a letter to Councilmember Hoyt, with a copy to Mayor Fraser, expressing "dissent and dismay" at Fraser's veto because he didn't permit the courts to rule on the constitutionality of the ordinance. Tribe articulated his reasoning:

> This veto is an abuse of the fundamental structure of our system of government. In the name of not passing the buck to the courts, a view with which I am in general sympathetic, the Mayor has acted unilaterally to deprive the courts of their unique Constitutional func-

tion, to pass on legislation that is not obviously unconstitutional. Hiding behind the First Amendment in the face of this novel measure, whose supposed in validity follows surely from no clear precedent, the Mayor has usurped the judicial function.

While many hard questions of conflicting rights will face any court that confronts challenges to the ordinance, as drafted its rests on a rationale that closely parallels many previously accepted exceptions to justly stringent First Amendment guarantees. While remaining uncertain myself as to the ultimate outcome of a judicial test, I urge you not to allow an executive to prevent the courts from adjudicating what may eventually be found to be the first sensible approach to an area which has vexed some of the best legal minds for decades.[9]

Four months later on May 1, 1984, Tribe sent a similar letter directly to Mayor Fraser:

While I am prepared to assume that you acted from a good faith assessment of your constitutional duties, I cannot share Professor Dershowitz's admiration for the role you chose to play in interposing yourself so preemptively between those who believe their rights are being violated by anti-female pornography, and the courts—which alone can fairly decide whether this proposed protection of those alleged rights can be reconciled with the transcendent importance of free speech in an open society.[10]

Tribe's letters are puzzling and troubling. They suggest that any proposal passed by a municipal, state, or federal legislative body, so long as the bill is not "obviously" unconstitutional, is appropriate for passage and entitled to federal court review as part of the courts' "unique constitutional function." Tribe thus appears to adopt the most extreme version of Morgan's "judicial monopoly" approach and condemns the holder of executive office, whether president, governor, or mayor, as an abuser of the "fundamental structure of our system of government" when he or she exercises the executive veto power based on a belief that the legislation awaiting signature contains constitutional flaws.

Throughout this nation's history there have been varying views as to which branch or branches of government is the repository of the ultimate decision regarding the constitutionality of a given piece of legislation. No serious suggestion has been made, however, that the executive branch—when granted the veto power—may not freely exercise that right. Certainly, if the executive can exercise the veto power based on dislike of or disagreement with the substance of a legislative act, it would not make sense to say that a veto based on the belief that the legislative act conflicts with the Constitution is an "abuse."[11] Thus, assuming, as even Tribe is willing to do, that Mayor Fraser's First Amendment concerns were genuine (and, in fact, the federal courts vindicated his view when they struck down the similar Indianapolis ordinance drafted by MacKinnon and Dworkin), the charge of judicial usurpation by "hiding behind the First Amendment" does not seem to be fair.

In any event, Mayor Fraser had vetoed the amendment on January 5, 1984. A week later, the city council failed to override the veto, with only five of the thirteen council members voting in favor of the bill. (Five of the thirteen members were new to the council.) At the same time, the council created a task force, composed of the mayor, three city council members, two civil rights commissioners, and one representative each from the library board and from the arts commission to consider the issue. Some months later, after hearings that included a far broader representation of community views, the task force came up with a recommendation for zoning and nuisance laws, revision of certain criminal laws, and a very much weakened and limited version of the MacKinnon/Dworkin proposal. The task force had received two legal opinions from the city attorney. The first concluded that, under Minnesota state law, the city of Minneapolis (as opposed to the state of Minnesota) did not have the power to create a private cause of action, permitting persons harmed by pornography to sue the producers and sellers of the material.[12] In the second, taking a broader look at the constitutionality of the entire bill, the city attorney concluded a twenty-two-page opinion by finding, "Because the proposed ordinance does not direct itself at conduct that is within government control and impacts so directly upon protected expression, a Court would probably find that it is overbroad. Because the proposed ordinance's key terms are undefined and allow broad, subjective interpretation of its coverage, a Court would probably find that the ordinance is vague."[13] This opinion subsequently was proven to be accurate.

When the city council committee received the task force's report, it substituted a slightly modified version of the original MacKinnon/Dworkin amendment for the very much more limited version that had cleared the task force. The council then adopted the revised proposal. After a period of public discussion and further demonstrations, the city council passed the MacKinnon/Dworkin version of the proposal, by a vote of 7-6. Once again Mayor Fraser vetoed, and once again the council failed to override the veto.

The original passage of the Minneapolis ordinance and its veto by Mayor Fraser had attained a significant amount of publicity throughout the country. After Mayor Fraser's veto had been roundly criticized by Tribe, early in 1984 Mayor

William Hudnut of Indianapolis, Indiana, and Indianapolis City Council Member Beulah Coughenour met Charlee Hoyt at a convention. They discussed the MacKinnon/Dworkin proposal and its status. As a result, discussions were initiated between Coughenour, the Indianapolis city attorney's office and the county prosecutor's office. MacKinnon was asked to assist.

A split developed among the various Indianapolis municipal legal advisors. The chief prosecutor was strongly in favor of the proposal as it had originally been presented in Minneapolis. On the other hand, both the city attorney's office and the attorney for the city council believed that, unless substantial modifications were made, the proposal would not withstand constitutional scrutiny. In March 1984, two lawyers in the city attorney's office advised Mayor Hudnut that the ordinance as proposed in Minneapolis was constitutionally defective. They suggested using Professor Tribe's recommendation to narrow the scope of the proposal by limiting it to pictorial depictions of explicit violence and physical abuse.[14] When, however, these lawyers were asked to meet with the administration committee of the council, which was the committee considering the proposal, the lawyers inexplicably spoke only of how the ordinance could be defended, if passed, and not of the proposal's constitutional infirmities.

Similarly, when the committee began considering a somewhat modified version of the original Minneapolis model, the counsel to the council—an attorney specifically designated to advise it on legal matters and therefore presumably responsive to its needs—was not ready to give his opinion, saying that he would need a number of weeks to render a formal opinion, weeks that the proponents of the ordinance were not willing to provide. Nor did he appear anxious to render an opinion on this politically sensitive issue.

Rather he reminded the committee that even the Supreme Court justices are not unanimous in most of the First Amendment cases that they decide, and therefore his legal opinion might not be helpful.

The reluctance of the municipal attorneys to stand in the way of an apparently popular approach to a controversial issue is understandable, given the political pressure; nevertheless their failure to do their job is troubling. The attorneys' failure to provide their client, the council, with guidance left the council legally adrift, with Professor MacKinnon as the only life preserver. One council member stated his frustration: "I think it is extremely significant that[,] in the draft of the ordinance itself[,] the persons that had the legal minds . . . found it necessary to pin the comment on the ordinance that it had not been tested for constitutionality, and that they were not comfortable with it. *I have not seen that on other ordinances.* As a matter of fact, constitutionality is *always a test* for creating an ordinance in the first place. . . . They [city lawyers] did not want their professional integrity impugned."[15]

Once again, as in Minneapolis, the matter moved with haste and without full discussion by all interested participants, although in this case there was, as noted, consultation with the municipality's legal advisors. The hearings before the administration committee lasted just over four hours.[16] MacKinnon spoke first, at considerable length, followed by anecdotal witnesses who described particular incidents extensively, and followed finally by the prosecutors. No scheduled witnesses objected to or questioned any aspect of the proposal. Only when the members of the public were given an opportunity to testify did persons raise objections and questions. Thus we again see the legislative fact-finding role skewed and converted from a process to elicit information to one of unqualified public endorsement.

At the end of the hearing on April 16, 1984, after some attempts to postpone the matter, the proposed ordinance was referred by the administration committee to the full city council. Four days later the entire city council held hearings. The council chamber was packed with media and spectators. The Reverend Greg Dixon, a founder of the Moral Majority and minister of the Baptist Temple in Indianapolis, and the organization Citizens for Decency through Law brought supporters of the bill in busloads to the hearing. Although it had previously stated that it would have no witnesses, the council shifted gears on the day of the meeting and had a lengthy introduction by MacKinnon. This was followed by scientific evidence from Professor Edward Donnerstein as to the causal relationship of pornography to harm to women. After three statements by persons objecting to the proposal who had been asked to testify at the last minute, the council voted, and by an overwhelming vote of 24-5 passed the MacKinnon proposal.

On May 1, 1984, Mayor Hudnut signed the ordinance. On that same day a lawsuit challenging the law, which had been threatened by various media groups, was brought in the federal district court in Indianapolis by a group of plaintiffs, including an Indianapolis video store chain, a television programming distributor, an Indiana book and periodical wholesaler, individual readers, and trade associations of booksellers, college stores, book publishers, librarians, wholesalers, and distributors.

Speaking on NBC's *Today* show on May 17, 1984, Hudnut justified his approval of the ordinance that Minneapolis Mayor Fraser had vetoed. He articulated a view similar to the one that Tribe included in his letter to Mayor Fraser:

> One of the reasons why I signed it [the MacKinnon ordinance] is that, as a representative of the executive

branch of government, I'm not the judge and I'm not the jury and I don't think I should prejudge the constitutionality of this. I think that it is worth a try and I'd like to take it all the way to the Supreme Court. Maybe the Supreme Court would add a fifth definition or restraint that helps to restrict First Amendment rights.[17]

Earlier in the same interview, Mayor Hudnut suggested that using the judiciary as a sounding board in this way was part of the "constitutional process."

And Councilwoman Coughenour, the leader in passing the MacKinnon/Dworkin proposal in Indianapolis, was quoted as viewing the possibility of unconstitutionality "philosophically" when the court challenge began:

> The first plane the Wright brothers made didn't fly. Now we've gone to the moon. You have to start somewhere. If for some reason the court finds the ordinance flawed and sends it back on technical grounds, but says the concept is still valid, then we'll know better how to try it again.
>
> This is a beginning. With every beginning there's hope, I guess.[18]

Faced with a lawsuit spelling out specific alleged constitutional defects in the ordinance, the city and its counsel reconsidered certain of the provisions. Clarifications and modifications were proposed and passed by the council. At the same time, however, symbolizing the tension between trying to make the law "more constitutional" and trying to achieve the aims of its more vocal adherents, a new provision was added that raised further constitutional issues.

In court the ordinance did not fare well. On May 9, 1984, a week after the suit had been brought, the ordinance was preliminarily enjoined by a federal district judge. On

November 19, 1984, it was held unconstitutional, a decision that was unanimously upheld by a three-judge federal appellate court the next year. When the city appealed to the United States Supreme Court, that court refused to take the case on full briefing and summarily affirmed the lower court decisions.[19]

The challenge to the constitutionality of the Indianapolis municipal ordinance had been brought in the federal court pursuant to a federal statute, Section 1983 of Title 42 of the United States Code, which authorizes suits to be brought against state officials who are depriving citizens of their rights under the federal constitution "under color of state law." Although when its predecessor was originally passed as § 1 of the Civil Rights Act of 1871 it was an outgrowth of the recent Civil War, Section 1983 has become the major jurisdictional method for challenging actions by the states and their representatives in the federal courts. Only five sections later, § 1988, is a provision for the reimbursement of legal fees and litigation expenses of the prevailing party by the losing party. (While British law provides for the loser to pay the winner's legal fees as a matter of course, American jurisprudence has viewed this as an impediment to access to the courts by those without considerable means. Thus, in the United States, each side generally bears its own costs. A suit brought alleging state infringement of federal constitutional rights was seen as an appropriate exception to the rule. Interestingly enough, in such a case the ability of a successful plaintiff to recover his or her costs was seen as encouraging, rather than discouraging, such access.[20]) Although Indianapolis contested and litigated the claims for reimbursement, the groups that successfully challenged the constitutionality of the MacKinnon/Dworkin ordinance were awarded over $100,000, which was paid by the city of Indianapolis.

The Supreme Court's 1985 order did not end the saga. MacKinnon has continued to press for enactment of the proposal by states and municipalities throughout the country. For example, in November 1985 a proposition to enact the proposal was on the ballot in Cambridge, Massachusetts, and was defeated. The subsequent Bellingham, Washington, offspring of the MacKinnon/Dworkin proposal provides yet another view of responsibility for the constitutionality of legislative acts. In Bellingham it was citizens legislating at the ballot box through an initiative who enacted a clearly unconstitutional law. In the fall of 1988, a group of Bellingham, Washington, voters, motivated by CROW (Civil Rights Organizing for Women), a feminist organization locally based at Western Washington State University, placed on the ballot in the city, in accordance with the Bellingham charter's right to legislate by citizen initiative, a proposal substantially the same as the Indianapolis ordinance that had already been found unconstitutional by the federal courts (a decision that had been affirmed by the United States Supreme Court). Thus the situation was significantly different from that faced by the Indianapolis City Council and its legal advisors. While at the time of the Indianapolis proceeding MacKinnon and her supporters could contend that the proposal should, in the future, be held constitutional, it was indisputable that under precedent as it existed at the time of the Bellingham vote the proposal was not constitutional. The city, recognizing the problem, sought to avoid the costs of future litigation by opposing the initiative and seeking to have it kept off the ballot. The state superior court held that the city could not prevent the vote.[21] The initiative was adopted by the electorate, despite attempts by public officials to highlight the fact that it already had been declared unconstitutional.

After passage, a suit was brought to have it declared

unconstitutional based on the earlier precedents. Since the city of Bellingham would not deny the ordinance's unconstitutionality, a number of interested citizens were permitted to intervene to participate in the case. Based on the Supreme Court decision, the federal court struck down the ordinance.[22] Then came the interesting question of whether the plaintiffs, a Bellingham bookstore, a local poet, a local writer, and various trade associations, would be reimbursed for their expenses in having the ordinance struck down again. The city argued that it had done everything it could. The plaintiffs argued that the city should be held liable for the actions of its voters, just as Indianapolis had been held liable for the actions of its mayor and city council. The court did award reimbursement of fees and expenses, stating, "The City of Bellingham argues that special circumstances are present because it demonstrated in good faith in opposing the initiative. . . . It is true that the City Council opposed placing the initiative on the ballot. However, as the plaintiffs point out, the voters *are* the City."[23]

The events that occurred in each of the three jurisdictions in connection with their consideration of the MacKinnon/Dworkin proposed ordinance raise three common issues. The first relates to how the legislative body is to inform itself about the constitutional issues that are raised by a bill. Part of the process is to conduct hearings as to the facts that require legislative relief, the appropriate nature of such relief, and, if relevant, the constitutional issues raised by the proposal. An orchestrated, accelerated legislative hearing process does not provide an appropriate forum for the consideration of legislative issues, especially when they have constitutional dimensions. Most constitutional issues have gray components. A facially plausible argument for constitutionality can be developed for most unconstitutional legislation. Critical analysis is often required to expose the fallacies or weaknesses of such an argument. And critical analysis often takes time; time to develop, time to expound, and time to be understood. This factor underlies the complicated procedures some states require to amend their constitutions or other basic laws. An amendment to the New York State Constitution, for example, requires passage by two successive legislatures and then the approval of the electorate at a general election. There generally is no such requirement for the passage of ordinary legislation, constitutional or not. And such time and reflection were not part of the legislative process in Minneapolis, Indianapolis, or Bellingham.

The highly charged atmosphere in all three cities contributed to the legislators' failure to deal appropriately with the constitutional issues. Issues of gender, religion, morality, and politics combined to create a momentum and milieu that discouraged serious critical consideration. Raising serious constitutional issues was seen as a political tactic; thus the underlying substance was belittled and the need to respond diminished. (Persons raising constitutional issues often desire the defeat of the proposed legislation both because they believe it is unconstitutional and the passage of unconstitutional legislation is bad and because they believe that the aims of the proposed legislation are harmful. Those raising these issues may in fact have difficult separating these two rationales. However, that does not mean, as is often asserted, that the constitutional issues are not meritorious, or that they are not made in good faith.)

Politics in the traditional sense of the word also negatively affected the deliberative process and limited a more critical consideration of the constitutional issues. In Minneapolis, women's issues, as well as concern about control of what many perceived to be quality-of-life issues, combined with the imminent departure of a significant portion of the city council to impose an unnaturally rapid time schedule on the process. In Indianapolis, conservative religious pressure combined with a desire to be a leader in the enactment of an attractive new mode of controlling an unwelcome civic companion had a similar effect. In both cases, serious critical legal review by others than the proponents of the legislation was absent. One must be careful, however, when bemoaning haste and the impact of undue political pressures. Popular sovereignty and civic participation are the essence of democracy, and a democracy need not always be tidy to be just. Haste in the consideration of the ordinances in Minneapolis and Indianapolis did not further democracy. The one-sided, programmed hearings created an unbalanced picture of the issue for both council members and citizens in general. In addition, they discouraged those with dissenting views from presenting their views publicly.

The Minneapolis and Indianapolis experiences once again demonstrate the importance to responsible legislation of fact-finding hearings actually intended to examine and consider the facts, as well as the necessity, even—or perhaps, especially—in the face of heightened political pressure, for serious legislative attention to constitutional concerns with the assistance of objective counsel. Speed may often be politically advantageous; for one thing, it keeps the opposition off guard. It can also, however, prevent comprehensive fact-finding and responsible consideration of constitutional issues.

The second issue raised is how to select from differing views of the legal "experts." Should the legal opinion of expert counsel be accepted as final? Both the Minneapolis and Indianapolis city councils had few, if any, lawyers as members. They relied on the opinion of the renowned legal scholar who had written the proposed ordinance and who had presented it to the councils for their consideration and, she hoped, their approval. As Councilmember Charlee Hoyt, the major proponent of the proposal in Minneapolis, put it, MacKinnon and Dworkin's "in-depth review and knowledge of the *latest*, most up-to-date research on the effects of pornography and of the court cases involving pornography, which they developed for teaching th[eir] class, made them eminently qualified to serve as consultants in the development of th[e] ordinance,"[24] —and, presumably, consultants regarding its constitutionality as well.

But MacKinnon was the proponent of this new approach. The creator of a novel legal approach, like all creators, having invested intellectual capital in the idea is unlikely to be an objective critic. In the scientific arena, replication by an independent researcher is required to validate a thesis. Can the same concept be applied in the constitutional arena? I think not. On the other hand, the legal and administrative bureaucracy, when faced with a radical proposal, may well reflect a bias in favor of the status quo and be reluctant to analyze the new idea neutrally. It is difficult for a legislative body that, like the Minneapolis and Indianapolis city councils, does not include legal scholars to make an informed decision on constitutional issues, particularly when it has not received guidance from an advisor known to it. Legislative bodies with members who have a constitutional law legal background, for example United States Senators Wayne Morse (a former law professor) and Howell Heflin (previously chief justice of the Alabama Supreme Court), may come to rely on those members because of their expertise. A legislative body, when considering whether to enter uncharted or murky constitutional waters, must seriously consider the issues of constitutionality that are raised. Certainly this requires more than reliance on the proponent of the proposal. Rather it requires advice from one or more persons with knowledge, experience, and objectivity, whether that person be an attorney in the executive branch, a legislative counsel, an academic scholar, or a fellow legislator.

This raises again the question of to whom a legislator seeking knowledgeable and impartial advice can turn. Is there really such a thing as "impartial" advice when the issue relates to highly political issues of the day? It is difficult, for example, to separate the constitutional issues raised by legislation relating to abortion, flag burning, hate speech, pornography, or religion in the public sphere from the emotional and political (in the nonparty sense of the word) components of those issues. While it is often not easy for the legislator to separate sound objective advice from that given to advance a cause, in the absence of sound advice, a conscientious legislator has nowhere to turn with comfort, and a legislator with an agenda has the ability to obscure substantial constitutional infirmities. While independent legislative counsel may combine lack of bias with lack of expertise, such counsel can and should consider the arguments made by those with expertise, pro and con, and independently evaluate the merits of the arguments or seek others to evaluate them.

The Indianapolis administration committee and city council hearings graphically highlight the difficulties legislators face when dealing with issues of constitutionality. Lawyers spoke both for and against the constitutionality of the proposal. The proponent of the new approach was a highly regarded law professor whose reputation was based in great part on the development of a now generally accepted "new approach" in the area of sexual harassment. If that new approach had been found valid, why not this? On the other hand, as Councilmember Shaw plaintively asked, "[MacKinnon's] the expert; but where is *our* expert?" Similarly Councilmember McGrath was of the view that all those who had testified were biased—presumably since they were either speaking in favor or against the proposal—while the city attorney would be unbiased. (McGrath, who was not a supporter of the proposal, may well have had expectations that the city attorney's position would not be supportive of the proposal. McGrath did not refer to the prosecutor's office. Debbie Daniels of that office had been working with Councilmember Coughenour on preparing the proposal. It was Coughenour who referred to Daniels's views.)

Constitutionality is—or at least has become—a particular province of the lawyers. One would expect, therefore, that the availability of independent, unbiased counsel to advise the legislators would be desirable, perhaps even required. Indianapolis Councilmember Shaw's cry—"Where is *our* expert?" was justified. This was particularly touching given the fact that, in Indianapolis, the council has its own attorney. But the council's attorney was reluctant to take a position, the city attorney expressed his concerns "off the record," and the prosecutor's office was supportive of the proposal and had participated in its drafting. It is little wonder that the views of the highly credentialed, articulate author and proponent of the ordinance had so much influence. In Minneapolis, on the other hand, the attorneys for the various governmental agencies affected, likely to be critical of the ordinance, were basically excluded from the legislative process.

The third issue raised by the three examples is how a legislator can responsibly consider new approaches to the solution of problems that raise constitutional concerns or that may require reexamination of existing constitutional precedents. The issue was raised by Professor Tribe's letters to Minneapolis officials, by Mayor Hudnut's statement in support of his signing the ordinance into law that he should not "prejudge" its constitutionality, and by Councilmember Coughenour's statement that this was a "beginning" and that "with every beginning there's hope."

Tribe's concern that the veto would prevent the courts from considering the constitutionality of an interesting new approach is an argument often heard in response to contentions that proposed legislation is unconstitutional under then existing and ruling Supreme Court precedents. Some have countered that test litigation can usually reopen issues, pointing to the series of lawsuits culminating in *Brown v. Board of Education*,[25] resulting in the overruling of *Plessy v. Ferguson*,[26] which had established the concept of "equal but separate accommodations for the white and colored races." However that approach to raising constitutional issues is workable only in certain types of situations, such as when governmental action or inaction, or an existing statute as in the school segregation cases, is challenged as violating the Constitution or when a governmental response to civil disobedience provides a governmental forum for constitutional resolution.

The MacKinnon/Dworkin approach was not claimed to be constitutionally required. Rather the proposal was put forward as a way of resolving what MacKinnon and Dworkin perceived as a societal fault or inequity. Thus a lawsuit to require a government to implement the approach would have been promptly dismissed. Such a suit, to be successful, would have required a court to make three determinations:

1. That a societal fault or inequity exists that needs to be remedied;
2. That the suggested remedy is either the best or, at least, an acceptable remedy;
3. That the suggested remedy is constitutional.

Although at times courts are required to make findings similar to the first two of these determinations in the context of adversary litigation, courts are not well equipped to do so. Rather, policy making and fact-finding are considered to be the forte of legislatures. While the third determination sounds "judicial" in nature, when it is separated from a specific controversy, it raises a number of serious questions. For example, were proponents of legislation to bring such an action, who would choose those to argue against it and how would they be chosen?[27]

Finally, the relationship of political pressures to legislative decisions on constitutionality should be noted. Repeatedly, councilmembers in both cities bemoaned the fact that, despite doubts about the constitutionality of the proposal, voting against the proposal left them open to charges that they were soft on, or, even worse, supporters of, pornography.

I believed then when I litigated the challenge to the Indianapolis ordinance, and I believe even more strongly now, that the MacKinnon/Dworkin proposal is unconstitutional and that it was correctly decided by the courts. In my opinion, had there been full and fair hearings covering both the factual premises and the constitutional issues raised, it is likely that the proposal would not have been adopted. But if full and fair hearings had been held, and had the councilmembers nevertheless, after consideration of the testimony, voted for the proposal, they should not have been faulted. Responsible legislation does not mean that the correct choice is always made.

4

A Constitution-Proof Law

The impact of a dedicated and tenacious "constitutional expert" in procuring the passage of unconstitutional legislation when the legislature considers the legislation politically or ideologically beneficial cannot be overestimated. In the Minneapolis and Indianapolis hearings on the civil antipornography ordinance, discussed at length in chapter 3, the ability of the proponents of the ordinance to quote and personally present Catharine MacKinnon, both author and advocate of the ordinance, was a trump card in the debates prior to passage of the ordinance. A similar situation occurred in 1977–78 in Tennessee, although the expert, Larry Parrish, was less well-credentialed than MacKinnon.

Tennessee, like Minnesota, is a state in which the legislature has had difficulty developing laws regulating explicit sexual material that are constitutionally permissible. In part this may be because the citizens of Tennessee have a large, politically active conservative religious component whose members view this issue as both a moral and legal problem to be dealt with, a view often reflected in the legislature.

Larry Parrish was well known in Memphis. While an assistant U.S. attorney in Memphis, he had spearheaded an antiobscenity drive that featured numerous prosecutions, including the successful prosecution of Harry Reems and other actors in the movie *Deep Throat*. Parrish did not have a reputation as a constitutional law expert; nor did he have MacKinnon's national academic renown. However, Parrish had developed a reputation as an effective crime fighter with a particular focus: obscene sexually explicit materials. After Parrish left the U.S. attorney's office in 1977, he began to express publicly his dissatisfaction with Tennessee's obscenity laws. In June 1977 he told a broadcasting group that he suspected that the obscenity laws then in effect were written by the attorneys for distributors of "adult" magazines and movies. He said, "The people who are distributing pornography want a law forbidding their activity. It provides a forum for them," and that the problem could be solved by a "few strict laws eliminating the vagueness in current laws and a few tough prosecutions."[1] Later that year, Parrish, having obtained the financial and political support of an array of religious and antipornography organizations, sought to solve the problem by drafting a proposed obscenity law based on what he described as "exhaustive legal research combined with the experience of hundreds of hours of investigative and trial experience."[2] Parrish's proposal was intended to substitute for the then existing Tennessee obscenity statutes.

The proposed law was complex and unusual. A defendant charged with disseminating obscene material could not plead guilty and was required to be tried by a jury. The trial was to be given the highest priority over all other cases, including capital cases. A defendant was required to post a bond equal to whichever was less—$100,000 or the potential fine if found guilty. The penalty for a first offense would be six months in prison and a fine equal to the defendant's gross income from all sources for one year, plus all of the costs of the government's investigation, prosecution, trial, and appeal. A convicted defendant could escape the costs of the government's investigation and the trial, if at the commencement of the trial the defendant informed the judge that he or she would have pleaded guilty if she or he had been permitted to do so, and if thereafter the defendant introduced no evidence, conducted no cross-examination, and did not participate in any manner in the trial other than being physically present. After such a trial, any material adjudged obscene by a single jury would be contraband throughout the state and could be seized and destroyed.

Parrish's proposed statute was far longer than other comparable statutes. In order to create what he called a "Constitution-proof" law, Parrish drafted the definitional provisions of the statute using actual language taken from Supreme Court and other appellate court decisions. His intent was to achieve specificity by using language from court decisions, the "sacred sources"; the result was a lengthy, wordy, difficult-to-understand proposed statute. Parrish justified the proposal, saying,

> The statutory scheme [is] proposed to deal with the current problem concerning the proliferation of obscenity in society. . . . One should not be misled by the length of the statutory scheme. That is, the length is necessary to provide the detailed specificity to insure that constitutionally protected forms of communication may not be drawn into suspect[sic] and to eliminate that which is obscene effectively. In other words, the breadth

of the statutory scheme may not be measured by its length. Also, the statutory scheme is so drawn that vagueness, which is a common problem in such legislation, if not eliminated, is reduced to an absolute de minimis amount.[3]

This attempt to achieve specificity by using extensive quotes from and paraphrasing Supreme Court and other court decisions resulted in verbosity and its own form of vagueness, akin to incomprehensibility. For example, "average person" was defined as "a hypothetical human being whose attitude represents a synthesis and composite of all of the various attitudes of all individuals in society at large which attitude is the result of common human experience, understanding development, culturalization and socialization in the United States, taking into account relevant factors which affect and contribute to that attitude, limited to that which is personally acceptable, as opposed to, that which might merely be tolerated."

Parrish had obtained and organized the support of religious and politically conservative groups, including Citizens Against Pornography, Citizens for Decency through Law, and the Memphis Leadership Foundation. Parrish presented the bill to the legislature "with as near an absolute guarantee of constitutionality as any statute on any subject could have.... It welcomes challenge at any level from any perspective."[4] His "guarantee" was to be significant to the Tennessee legislature in light of a history of Tennessee obscenity laws that ran afoul of constitutional protections for speech. Finally, Parrish was quoted as saying that the bill was "so tough it would do away with obscenity."[5]

The Parrish bill was initially considered by a Joint Special Committee on Obscenity of the Tennessee legislature. The committee received about fifteen hundred to two thousand letters urging passage of the bill in addition to being pressured by lobbying groups, which sent representatives to committee meetings, including the meeting at which the committee voted to forward the proposal to the House and Senate Judiciary Committees.[6] When the bill, which was entitled the Tennessee Obscenity Act of 1978, got to those committees in January 1978 it was expected to die. As reported in a Nashville paper,

> "That's what needs to happen to this bill," one lawmaker says privately, "a nice quiet death."
>
> However solons say they're under immense political pressure for [sic] church-affiliated organizations to vote in favor of the measure. "And this is an election year," one notes. "You can't explain to these people that this is bad legislation. But how can you vote against it?"[7]

Pressure from Parrish, the religious groups, and a few key senators kept the bill moving, although various constitutional issues had been raised. The chairman of the legislative committee of the Tennessee District Attorneys General Conference wrote, "The only opposition expressed by some district attorneys to the proposed bill concerned the constitutionality of a large number of provisions," as well as the practical problems arising from the prohibition against plea bargaining and pleading guilty.[8]

To deflect part of the constitutional concern, Senator Ben Atchley, a major sponsor of the bill, requested a legal opinion from the attorney general of Tennessee. The Tennessee attorney general's is an unusual post. Most attorneys general are either appointed by the governor or elected by the citizens of the state. In Tennessee the attorney general is appointed by its supreme court for an eight-year term.[9] Thus, its attorney general is likely to be more removed from political concerns than one would be who had been elected or had been appointed by an elected governor. Under Tennessee law, the attorney general is required to be responsive to the needs of the legislature. One of the statutorily mandated duties of the attorney general is "to give . . . members of the general assembly, when called upon, written legal opinions." The statute further states, recognizing that the legislative process will not necessarily halt while the attorney general ponders legal or constitutional issues, that "[i]t is the legislative intent that when a request for a written legal opinion is from a member of the general assembly and concerns pending legislation, such request shall be replied to as expeditiously as possible."[10]

Senator Atchley's request to the attorney general was limited to seeking advice regarding the constitutionality of only three specific portions of the proposal: the search and seizure provisions, the prohibition on pleading guilty, and the monetary penalties imposed on a convicted defendant relating to costs imposed on a convicted defendant who presented a defense at trial. Meanwhile, the political and lobbying pressures grew. The lieutenant governor, apparently anticipating the attorney general's opinion, indicated concern that the bill could pass, "even with provisions declared unconstitutional by the state attorney general," because of "a head of steam" building.[11] At the same time, legislators were receiving hundreds of identical letters urging that the Parrish bill be passed in its original form without any amendments.

Complying with the statutory-promptness requirement, the attorney general's office issued its legal opinion on February 6, 1978. The letter did not provide the crisp "yes-or-no" type of answer that Senator Atchley probably desired. Rather, C. Hayes Cooney, the chief deputy attorney general, wrote that the search and seizure provisions raised constitutional questions, the prohibition on pleading guilty raised an issue as to which the attorney general's office "found no cases directly . . . on point, but recognize that litigation on this point may be forthcoming," and the penalty for not pleading guilty raised "a serious constitutional question." Interestingly enough, Cooney went on to mention that a provision about which he had not been asked—the monetary fine equal to gross income from all sources—raised constitutional questions of excessiveness and disproportioness. Finally, the attorney general's office gratuitously suggested that, since obscenity legislation was particularly subject to attack, it might be a better policy to simply amend the existing Tennessee law, which had been held constitutional, "to alleviate prosecutorial problems."

Despite the fact that the opinion appears on its face not to have taken a firm position on constitutionality, one Nashville paper read the letter as an opinion that several sections of the bill were unconstitutional; the other paper read the letter as questioning the constitutionality of several provisions.[12] A possible explanation for the difference between the opinion's language and the interpretation by both of the newspapers is that part of the attorney general's message was between the lines, understood only by those familiar with the usual language of similar prior communications. The unsought advice to reconsider the project might well be read in that light.

The fact that the attorney general responded to questions that were not asked in a communication that was, by its nature, either public or likely to become so, raises issues of concern. On the one hand, as attorney general of the state, it was his responsibility and perhaps obligation, to inform Senator Atchley of his constitutional concerns. On the other hand, the likelihood of a response more sweeping than the request could dampen the interest of legislators in making requests in the future. In balance, the response was appropriate. To respond only to the specific inquiry could well give third parties the mistaken impression that the attorney general was constitutionally comfortable with the bill as a whole.

Throughout February 1978, committee meetings and hearings were held on the Parrish proposal. Amendments were made, including deleting the ban on guilty pleas, reducing the fines to fixed amounts, and eliminating the provision imposing investigative costs on convicted defendants, "to temper the measure to an apparently constitutionally acceptable level."[13] Chief Deputy Attorney General Cooney was of the view that, even after the amendments, the legislation would be the subject of protracted litigation, with the likelihood of being struck down. He said, "I've studied the bill, and I still don't know what some of the definitions mean," he said.[14] Nevertheless, the proponents persevered. Just before the bill was to go before the general assembly for consideration, a conference was held between legislators and lobbyists for book, movie, periodical, and other media groups seeking to resolve some of the constitutional questions. But when a representative of the book and periodical groups argued that the contraband provision was unconstitutional, Senator Atchley replied, "That doesn't matter because if that section is declared unconstitutional, we have a severability clause that will keep the rest of the bill intact."[15] (A severability clause expresses the intent of the legislature that, if a provision of the statute is found to be invalid by reason of unconstitutionality, the entire statute is not to be stricken. Rather, the court is to carve out the invalid provision and uphold the remainder of the statute, if it is reasonably possible to do so.) The senator's reply is an excellent example of a significant abdication of the legislator's constitutional responsibility: simply referring a grab bag of provisions to the courts for them to sort out which ones are constitutionally viable.

On March 15, 1978, the Parrish bill, as amended, was passed by the Tennessee House of Representatives by a vote of 94-2, without any debate. Most of the legislators voting for the bill had not seen it in its final, amended form, a legislative fact that occurs all too often. According to a story in the *Nashville Banner,* Representative Charlie Ashford

> registered no vote at all on the bill, furiously complaining that he had been promised an opportunity to discuss the bill fully on the floor before acting on it.
>
> But that discussion never took place as the bill's sponsors . . . quickly cut off debate. . . .
>
> After the vote, Murray [one of the sponsors] conceded that there "might be a couple of places" where the bill "needs cleaning up a little," but said it was a good bill and a constitutional bill."[16]

Both Nashville newspapers, in reporting the passage, referred to the pressure exerted by the presence of several hundred conservative church-group members who came to Nashville "by busloads" to lobby for the bill and who were present in the chamber.[17]

The next week the bill passed the state senate by a vote of 29-4.

> About 180 anti-obscenity activists from across the state crammed the Senate galleries for the debate, and several senators said the measure has been the most intensively lobbied piece of legislation in the last several years.
>
> Some senators confided privately to reporters they believed the bill is unconstitutional and will be struck

down by the courts, but they were voting for it because of political pressure.[18]

Contrary to what had happened when the bill came up in the House, and probably because of the bad press that had received, there was a full debate in the Senate. After passage, the lobbyist for the district attorneys was still unhappy. He stated that it would be several years before the district attorneys would understand the bill well enough to enforce it because it was "so awkward and difficult to read."[19]

While Governor Blanton had initially expressed reservations about the Parrish bill because of constitutional questions, when it came to him after passage he signed it. As Blanton told Reverend J. Bazzel Mull, the radio evangelist to whom he first disclosed his intention to sign, the bill was not exactly what he wanted but he would sign it anyway because it was a step in the right direction.[20]

Only weeks later, a lawsuit challenging the statute was brought in the state court in Nashville by two Nashville bookstores, national trade associations representing booksellers, book publishers and college stores, and the Tennessee Library Association. (I was co-counsel in that action.) At about the same time, similar actions were brought in the state court in Memphis by two "adult" businesses targeted by the law and in the federal court in Knoxville. Under Tennessee law, when state officials are sued, the defendant is represented by the attorney general's office. In these cases the state was represented by Chief Deputy Attorney General C. Hayes Cooney, who had previously rendered his statutorily required opinion on the law he was now obligated to defend. Because of the delicacy of the potential conflict, as well as its political ramifications, Parrish, who had up to then been representing the church antipornography groups, was retained as special assistant to the attorney general.

On June 2, 1978, the Memphis judge held the statute unconstitutional, followed by a decision to the same effect in Nashville on July 7, 1978. In the Nashville case, the trial judge, Chancellor Robert S. Brandt, filed a scholarly sixty-one-page opinion,[21] the introduction of which summarized his holding:

> The Court concludes that most of the act is unconstitutional and that enforcement must be enjoined.
>
> Parts of the act are unintelligible and incomprehensible. Other passages are vague, obscure and unclear. The act does not conform to the requirements of the First Amendment to the United States Constitution as interpreted by the United States Supreme Court. Portions of the act clearly violate other parts of the United States Constitution and several provisions of the Tennessee Constitution. Much of the act cannot be implemented. Some sections are at variance with other laws and policies of the State of Tennessee.[22]

But Parrish was not daunted by the ruling. He said that although the Memphis judge was wrong "from top to bottom," he was pleased that now the entire matter could go to the Tennessee Supreme Court.[23] Referring to the subsequent Nashville ruling, Parrish said, "It's exactly what I expected, just judging from the comments he [the judge] made from the bench. But there is nothing he could say that could throw any doubt on the constitutionality of that law."[24]

Virtually every one of the points set out by Chancellor Brandt had been previously presented to the Tennessee legislature. Many of the issues had been discussed at length. And it was not only the "liberals" who had raised these issues. The attorney general's office had, somewhat gingerly perhaps, suggested that there were better ways to go. The district attorneys, with Cooney's concurrence, had, to the end, repeated the point that they didn't understand the provisions; in the language of Chancellor Brandt, portions of the law were unintelligible and incomprehensible. Why then had the legislature taken the irresponsible, reckless step of overwhelmingly approving this obviously defective statute? Most likely they did so because of the political pressures, the benefits from voting for the "elimination of obscenity" and the potential harm from voting against the bill.[25] It is hard to turn down the opportunity to pass a law that would banish obscenity and was "guaranteed" to pass constitutional muster. The legislature was, to a certain extent, merely going through the motions of a constitutional review. The general assembly did eliminate certain of the more egregious and unconstitutional provisions. But there was a limit to how far they could go without incurring the wrath of the groups supporting Parrish and his bill. Chief Deputy Attorney General Cooney's suggestion of simply amending the punishment provision did not satisfy the demand, encouraged by Parrish, for a new approach. In any event, as Senator Atchley had said, the bill had a severability clause that would let the courts excise any unconstitutional provisions from the law. He could have said that when such a court ruling occurred any displeasure of the proponents would be directed at the courts rather than at the senators and representatives.

Parrish appealed the case on behalf of the state to the Tennessee Supreme Court, which, after hearing oral argument, affirmed the ruling of unconstitutionality on May 6, 1979, and restored the prior obscenity statute. The court's ruling came "as a complete shock" to Parrish, who "definitely was not expecting it. . . . If the Supreme Court of the United States were given the opportunity to apply its holdings to this act, then I feel confident that it would uphold the statute."[26] Representative Scruggs, the sponsor of the bill in the House, also expressed surprise that the bill had been struck down.[27] While Parrish desired to seek further review from the United States Supreme Court, the governor and the attorney general decided not to go further. Thus ended the "guaranteed" Constitution-proof obscenity law. An appropriate epitaph would be this excerpt from an editorial the *Nashville Banner* published following the decision of the Tennessee Supreme Court:

> the process of making law deserves reflection here. One cannot escape the fact that . . . [the Tennessee Obscenity Act of 1978] was passed not only in response to pressure but passed by some with knowledge that it was bad law—with knowledge that courts eventually would resolve it while others, by their votes or reluctance to speak out clearly, took themselves off the political hook. That was last year. But such an example must always be troubling to a democratic society, particularly if the risk is knowingly run of infringing upon constitutional rights.[28]

5

If At First You Don't Succeed, Try, Try Again

When a statute has been held unconstitutional, obviously the legislature has the power and right to enact a corrective statute remedying the infirmity found by the court. If the policy underlying the invalidated statute is powerful, one could argue that the legislature has an obligation to reformulate the statute to cure the constitutional defect. Thus, when in 1972 the Supreme Court held unconstitutional death penalty statutes that permitted judges or juries to impose the penalty of death without standards to guide them in that duty,[1] many state legislatures rewrote their death penalty procedures to include constitutionally required standards. Although the new statutes raised some additional issues, the effort was basically a good faith attempt by the legislatures to develop procedures in accord with the constitutional requirements elucidated by the Supreme Court.

Even when a legislature enacts a revised law in good faith reasonably considering it to be constitutional, any further challenge to the law will result in litigation costs and uncertainty until the lawsuit is over. When, however, repeated efforts are made to craft a statute that will achieve that which has been prohibited by "sneaking by" the prior court decisions, the legislators are acting recklessly in violation of their constitutional oaths. Often in such cases an underlying legislative motive for passing a constitutionally flawed law is simply to extend the effectiveness of the scheme previously found unconstitutional, or, alternatively, to delay or defer the effectiveness of constitutionally mandated changes. Such legislative action breeds cynicism both in proponents of the legislation and in others. Proponents of the legislation are misled by the legislators into believing that they are actually doing something to resolve an issue or perceived problem. Others, even those not highly concerned by the substance of the legislation, become cynical because of the legislators' efforts to deal with an issue by obviously improper means.

The statutes that were passed in some southern states following the deconstitutionalization of segregated schools are examples of such legislative tactics.[2] More recently, Alabama's attempts to authorize school prayer can be cited.[3] But one need not look solely at the South. One recent egregious example of this type of lawmaking is the repeated attempts of the New York legislature to pass a law permitting the residents of the village of Kiryas Joel, New York, to establish a separate school district so that the children in the village who required special remedial education could take those courses in their own community separate from outsiders as required by their religious beliefs. Another example is the repeated attempts by the Missouri legislature to disqualify Planned Parenthood from eligibility for Missouri's state-funded family planning program because of the agency's use of private nongovernmental funds to endorse abortion and provide abortion services. Both of these examples are worth examining.

The Kiryas Joel School District

The issue of public funding of special education for the children of the village of Kiryas Joel has a history more than ten years long. Kiryas Joel is in Orange County, New York, approximately seventy miles northwest of New York City. It is a community of the Satmar sect of Hasidic Jews. The Satmars are politically influential in New York State, with their primary base in Williamsburg, Brooklyn. No one who is not a Satmar lives in Kiryas Joel, and separation of the sexes in social and public events is required. Yiddish is the principal language of Kiryas Joel; television, radio, and English-language publications are not in general use. The dress and appearance of the Satmar are distinctive; both males and females follow a prescribed dress code. Education is of special concern. Satmarer children generally do not attend public schools; instead, they attend their own religiously affiliated schools within the village. At school the children are separated by gender. The purpose of the separate religiously based educational system is to serve as a bastion against undesirable contact with the outside world and consequent acculturation or assimilation.

The jurisdiction of the Board of Education of the Monroe-Woodbury Central School District includes the village of Kiryas Joel, although, as noted, children of Kiryas Joel do not generally use the Monroe-Woodbury schools. In 1984 the board of education developed procedures with representatives of Kiryas Joel to provide remedial services to handicapped children at a "neutral site" within Kiryas Joel (actually an annex to one of the religious schools). But after two decisions of the United States Supreme Court in 1985 that held unconstitutional the delivery by the government of public education services in religious schools,[4] the board terminated the classes. That fall, the board of education brought an action in the New York state trial court seeking a declaration that it was not obligated to provide special education services except in public school buildings; Kiryas Joel counterclaimed for a declaration that the board was obligated to provide such services in the schools that the special education students regularly attended, namely the religious schools. Ultimately, the decision of the New York State Court of Appeals (the state's highest court) granted neither party the relief it sought.[5] The court held that the board was not restricted to offering such services in the public schools, but, at the same time, it was not required to provide them at the Kiryas Joel religiously based schools. This decision, leaving a resolution of the issue to the discretion of the Monroe-Woodbury School Board, which was not willing to offer the program other than in the public schools, did not settle the dispute.

One year later, on July 24, 1989, Governor Mario M. Cuomo signed a bill establishing a separate school district for the Village of Kiryas Joel. The bill had been passed earlier that month by the New York state legislature as chapter 748 of the Laws of 1989. The governor's memorandum approving the bill recognized that there were potential constitutional problems with the bill. He noted that "lawyers for the State Education Department argue[d] that the bill may be held unconstitutional."[6] The governor's counsel disagreed and advised that "on its face" that bill was constitutional.

Cuomo was persuaded by his counsel's view, and signed the bill.

The statute was clearly intended to solve a specific problem, the constitutional prohibition against the provision by the state of remedial services in the religious schools, for a specific entity, the Village of Kiryas Joel. In fact the statute runs squarely against the educational policy of the state, which was and is to eliminate smaller school districts and to create larger consolidated districts.[7] The impetus of the bill, thus, is similar to the impetus behind RFRA and the Omnibus Crime Control Act, to be discussed in chapter 6, in that it attempts to counteract the effects of decisions of the Supreme Court. However, chapter 748, rather than seeking a reversal of the *Aguilar* and *Grand Rapids School District* decisions in all or most of their applications, attempted to reverse only one specific factual application of those decisions.

Early in 1990, the New York State School Boards Association, its president, and its executive director brought an action in the New York state courts seeking a declaration that chapter 748 was unconstitutional on the ground that it violated the Establishment Clause of the First Amendment of the U.S. Constitution. After two years of litigation, the trial court held the law unconstitutional, finding that chapter 748 had the effect of advancing the religious beliefs of the Satmar religious group. That decision was upheld by the intermediate New York appellate court on December 31, 1992,[8] by the New York State Court of Appeals on July 6, 1993,[9] and on June 27, 1994, by the United States Supreme Court.[10] The Supreme Court held that the legislature had "singled out a particular religious sect for special treatment" in a "manner that fails to foreclose religious favoritism," thus violating the Establishment Clause of the First Amendment.[11] Comparing the creation of the school district to the process by which the Village of Kiryas Joel was formed pursuant to a religion-neutral law of general applicability, the Court stated: "Because the religious community of Kiryas Joel did not receive its new governmental authority [as a school board] simply as one of many communities eligible for equal treatment under a general law, we have no assurance that the next similarly situated group seeking a school district of its own will receive one."[12]

While concurring with the conclusion that 748 was unconstitutional, Justice O'Connor laid out a road map for the legislature to cure the unconstitutional aspects of the law:

> There is nothing improper about a legislative intention to accommodate a religious group, so long as it is implemented through generally applicable legislation. New York may, for instance, allow all villages to operate in their own [school] districts. If it does not want to act so broadly, it may set forth neutral criteria that a village must meet to have a school district of its own; these criteria can then be applied by a state agency and the decision would then be reviewable by the judiciary. A district created under a generally applicable scheme would be acceptable even though it coincides with a village that was consciously created by its voters as an enclave for their religious group.[13]

Only four days after the Supreme Court decision invalidating the statute creating the Village of Kiryas Joel School District, the New York legislature, seemingly following Justice O'Connor's road map, passed two separate but related laws. The problem facing the legislature was that it wanted to accommodate and resolve the Kiryas Joel problem while, at the same time, it wanted to retain its general policy against a multiplicity of smaller school districts. One of the hastily passed laws, chapter 279, expressly repealed chapter 748 and abolished the Kiryas Joel School District, but permitted the district to remain operational until either a state court ordered it to cease as a result of the Supreme Court decision, or until it was merged with or replaced by another school district established under article 31 of the New York State Education Law. The other new provision, chapter 241, amended article 31 of the Education Law to permit any municipality that met certain "neutral" qualifications to form its own school district. It should come as no surprise that Kiryas Joel met the qualifications; it promptly took the necessary steps to establish a new Kiryas Joel School District. Thus, five years after the school district was first established and two and a half years after its establishment was first held unconstitutional, the Kiryas Joel School District continued, and had, in effect, been given a statutory rebirth by the legislature.

While chapter 241 did appear to be of general application and religiously neutral, at the time it was passed, out of 1,546 municipalities in the state only Kiryas Joel met the statutorily mandated qualifications. Further, chapter 241 provided that subsequently chartered municipalities who might otherwise qualify were excluded from the benefits of the statute.

Once again, the New York State School Boards Association and its officers brought a suit in the New York state courts challenging the constitutionality of the two new statutes only weeks after they had been signed by the governor, claiming that the new statutes had the same intent and effect as chapter 748 and therefore were similarly unconstitutional. This demonstrates the importance of, and burdens on, private groups in limiting the harm created by the reckless passage of unconstitutional legislation. New York, unlike the federal government, has a statute that gives citizen taxpayers the right to challenge unconstitutional state legislation, and, if successful, to reimbursement of costs and expenses.[14] Nevertheless, prosecuting a suit against the state is time-consuming, costly, and hard work. It is often difficult to find a person or organization willing to shoulder the burden, even if they have a policy basis for the challenge. Thus the purported congressional override of the Supreme Court *Miranda* decision, discussed in chapter 6 of this book, was on the statute books for years without challenge; there are no associations of persons charged with criminal acts (or at least none that are willing to publicly declare themselves and become a plaintiff in such a challenge). Nevertheless, the School Boards Association, in 1994 again sensing a breach in the state's policy opposed to undersized school districts, stepped forward with its officers to challenge the law just as it had in 1989.

The New York trial court found the statute to be constitutional, focusing on the apparent facial neutrality of the qualifications.[15] However, the intermediate appellate court[16] and the state Court of Appeals[17] both found that the legislature had simply resurrected the prior law by using carefully crafted indirect means to achieve exactly the same result. As Judge Ciparick concluded for a unanimous Court of Appeals:

> [C]hapter 241 violates the Establishment Clause neutrality principles that form the core holding of *Kiryas Joel I* [the Supreme Court decision on chapter 748].... Notwithstanding its purported facial neutrality, we interpret chapter 241 as having the nonneutral effect of allowing the religious community of Kiryas Joel, but no other group at this time and probably ever, to create its own school district. Chapter 241's conferral of its special benefit on the Village of Kiryas Joel alone, as against virtually all other groups be they religious or nonreligious, effectively conveys a message of impermissible governmental endorsement of the Satmar community of Kiryas Joel.[18]

The court of appeals opinion was issued on May 6, 1997. Three months later, in August, the legislature tried again. Chapter 390 of Laws 1997, like chapter 241, set forth criteria for the establishment of new school boards. The criteria in chapter 390 were fewer and apparently easier to comply with. Senator Richard Dollinger, a Democrat from Rochester, cast the sole negative vote in the state senate, stating "What I think you have here is a situation where we, for some reason, are attempting to create a school district which we've been told by all our courts violates our First Amendment."[19] In response, Senator Emanuel Gold, a Democrat from Queens, forthrightly responded, "All this legislation is trying to do, Senator Dollinger, is exactly what you said. The courts have given us decisions that we don't like. We see a situation which needs us, and we are trying to find a way around it."[20]

When Governor George Pataki, who had defeated Cuomo, signed the bill, he stated that "this legislation truly is one of general applicability." Nathan Diament, director of the Institute for Public Affairs of the Union of Orthodox Congregations of America, supporters of the Kiryas Joel district, took the same approach. He said, "This statute is more broadly drawn than earlier versions that have been held unconstitutional. Although we believed the earlier versions of this legislation were constitutional, this revision will clearly challenge the courts to recognize that just because a generally drawn statute benefits a religious community or religious citizens that does not automatically make it constitutionally suspect."[21]

Once again the School Boards Association and its officers took up the cudgels and, for the third time, sued to challenge the constitutionality of a law intended to create or, by this time, to maintain, the Kiryas Joel School District. The legislature had attempted once again to set forth neutral standards that would accommodate the continuance of the Kiryas Joel School Board, while at the same time not opening the floodgates to a large number of economically, and probably educationally, inefficient small school districts. However, the New York state trial judge found that the legislators' third try would apply to only two communities, Kiryas Joel and Stony Point, also in Rockland County. As the *New York Times* explained the impact of the law in an editorial, "The reaction by Stony Point shows the danger of continuing any further down this road. Residents of that largely white district are circulating petitions to set up a school system separate from the more heavily minority neighborhoods around them."[22]

In his decision on April 2, 1998, the trial judge, Joseph C. Teresi, found that application to two communities was no better than application to one, particularly in the light of the history of the statute. The judge characterized the statute as "the third attempt of the Legislature of this state to ignore the rulings from courts at every level and to impermissibly endorse the Satmar community of Kiryas Joel."[23] The decision was affirmed only weeks later by the intermediate appellate court.[24]

Once again, the issue came to the New York Court of Appeals. On May 11, 1999, the court affirmed the ruling of unconstitutionality.[25] However, the decision was by a close vote of 4-3. Mayor Abraham Weider of Kiryas Joel was heartened by the dissent. "It's a 4-3 decision, which is better than it's ever been."[26] After an alternative attempt to create a special district under another law, which had been unused for eighty years, relief was sought from the U.S. Supreme Court, which application was pending when this chapter was written. At the same time, the legislature passed for the fourth time a statute which it hoped would continue the Kiryas Joel School District and pass constitutional muster.[27]

The legislators would likely characterize their actions differently than Judge Teresi did. They would argue that, when they passed the original law creating the Kiryas Joel School Board, although there were constitutional concerns and issues, the law was far from clearly invalid. Even the counsel to Governor Cuomo, and the governor himself, who is also a lawyer and former law clerk to a judge of the New York State Court of Appeals, thought it should be held constitutional. Then, when the initial law was held unconstitutional by the Supreme Court, the opinion of one of the justices had, in effect, laid out the path for constitutional legislative action. The subsequent statutes, the legislators would likely say, were attempts to do precisely what Justice O'Connor had suggested.

But an examination of these statutes shows attempts to craft legislation that facially complied with constitutional requirements by ostensibly allowing any community to set up its own public school board without actually doing so. However, the statutes as a practical matter authorized only the Kiryas Joel School District; it permitted as few other communities as possible to create their own new school boards. The single underlying goal of all the statutes was to authorize a religious community to have its own public school district that it could control and that would have access to public funds. The first statute dealt only with the Kiryas Joel board of education; the second was drafted in general terms but still only applied to the single community; the third applied to two municipalities (and possibly more in the future). Like a child who is told by its mother to walk immediately next to her and first takes one step toward its mother and then another, asking each time whether it is close enough, the New York legislature, recognizing that its real purpose was that clearly set forth in the original legislation, made revisions as narrowly as possible to see how little the courts would allow. Without hearings and without really focusing on the constitutional issue, the legislature, aided and abetted by the governor, pretended the legislation was something that it was not, a neutral law of general applicability.

It is not even clear that all members of the legislature who voted for the second and third bills were truly aware of the very narrow applicability of those bills. There is likely to be a difference between the level of the knowledge about proposed bills by the legislative leadership and those directly involved in the drafting and shepherding of a bill, on the one hand, and the remaining legislators who vote on the bill, on the other. When, as here, there are no hearings, those not in the inner circle are not likely to know much more about the bill than its general subject matter and whether their party's leadership is for or against passage. Even if there had been hearings, in many cases a hearing is not transcribed in a timely manner, if ever. Thus information disclosed at a hearing will not be readily available to those who did not attend the hearing. In this respect, yet another aspect of legislative irresponsibility and recklessness in dealing with constitutional issues can be the haste and lack of discussion even within the breadth of the legislature with which the issues are treated. The legislative memorandum describing the last of the statutes, chapter 390, includes no reference to potential constitutional issues or to the fact that two previous related statutes had been held unconstitutional; the governor's memorandum states that the constitutional defects have been cured.[28] The insiders, however, knew exactly what was going on; as was pointed out by the Appellate Division, the legislative summary published for the year 1997 referred to this as the "Kiryas Joel" law,[29] and the press release of the Institute of Public Affairs of the Orthodox Union (the umbrella organization of Orthodox Jewish synagogues) referred to the law as "legislation designed to leave in place the Kiryas Joel Village School District."[30]

The Kiryas Joel story had a group of sympathetic petitioners (the Satmar parents of children needing special or remedial education) who were part of a politically influential group, which sought to have a generally available educational benefit delivered in a way consistent with their religious sensibilities. In attempting to satisfy this request, the New York legislature disregarded the federal constitutional restraints against equal protection and establishment of religion and thereby garnered approval from this politically influential group. The courts were again placed in the role of the "bad guys," withholding the desired benefit, a benefit that the residents of Kiryas Joel, from their point of view, had every reason to expect would be provided. Further, for the past nine years, the burden has been on a not-for-profit trade association—the New York State School Boards Association—to spearhead the challenge to this series of unconstitutional laws when both legislature and governor have failed their constitutional obligations. Were it not for this association, the Kiryas Joel School Board might have remained unchallenged.

There is yet another interesting aspect to this story. It was the 1985 Supreme Court decision in *Aguilar v. Felton*[31] that resulted in the termination of the arrangement between the Monroe-Woodbury Central School District and the Village of Kiryas Joel for provision of remedial services at the village's religious school and led to the pressure for the separate school district. Twelve years later, in 1997, the Supreme Court reversed its *Aguilar* holding. In *Agostini v. Felton*[32] the Court held that the state's providing nonreligious educational services in a parochial school building does not violate the First Amendment. While it would seem that the *Agostini* decision would clear the way for the public school board to provide remedial special education at Kiryas Joel, the situation is not resolved. The Monroe-Woodbury School Board does not want to provide such services in the religious Kiryas Joel schools, and in 1985 the state Court of Appeals held that the Monroe-Woodbury board was not obligated to do so under then existing state law. Thus, the state for the third time unsuccessfully sought vindication in the state court of appeals (or the fourth time if one counts the 1985 decision) as to the constitutionality of the third statute attempting to establish the Kiryas Joel School Board.

It is worth noting that the legislature also disregarded potential state constitutional infirmities when it passed the four "Kiryas Joel" statutes. The New York State Constitution does not have an equivalent provision to the First Amendment Establishment clause. During the nineteenth century, certain public schools came under the de facto control of religious institutions. As a result, the 1894 Constitutional Convention adopted what is now Article XI, § 3, which bans the direct or indirect use of public funds to aid or maintain any school "wholly or in part under the control or direction of any religious denomination or in which any denomination tenet or doctrine is taught." The state constitutional issue will be decided based on a determination whether the domination, in fact, by the Satmar sect of the Kiryas Joel School Board constitutes "control or direction" for this purpose.

Missouri Family Planning Funds and Planned Parenthood

The next situation that we will consider demonstrates what a persistent and dedicated group of legislators, impelled by strong religious views against abortion, backed by effective lobbying, can do. They made numerous attempts to "punish" an organization with opposing views by preventing it from receiving state funding. Their efforts were repeatedly thwarted by established constitutional First Amendment and Fourteenth Amendment equal protection restrictions; the state cannot penalize persons or groups for exercising their First Amendment right to communicate their opinion. They nevertheless kept trying, and continue to do so.

Missouri is a state with a strong antiabortion prolife movement; it is the state from which arose the 1989 U.S. Supreme Court decision permitting the disbursement of state health funds to be conditioned on the requirement that no such funds be used for the provision of abortion services.[33] Commencing with its fiscal year 1993-94, Missouri appropriated funds for family planning services. The program had been proposed by Governor Mel Carnahan as a way of reducing the number of abortions.[34] In that fiscal year the appropriations bill provided that none of the appropriated family planning funds could be used "to perform or actively promote abortion as a method of family planning." The same condition was imposed for the 1994-95 fiscal year. In that year, Planned Parenthood of Mid-Missouri and Eastern Kansas, Inc., which segregated the government funds it received so that they would not be used for abortion services, received $207,018 of the total $1,093,029 appropriation.

The original appropriations bill for fiscal year 1995-96 continued the language of the prior years. However, the 1994 elections had brought a number of additional antiabortion members to the Missouri legislature. After the appropriations bill was presented in January, the Missouri Catholic Conference circulated an "Action Gram," urging its supporters to tell the Legislature, "in one, loud unified voice," that tax dollars should not go to Planned Parenthood because it "performs and promotes abortion."[35] From the outset of this campaign, it was clear that there was a First Amendment problem, because the attack was directed at a single agency,

Planned Parenthood, at least in part for the exercise of their constitutionally protected right to communicate proabortion views. The original amendment to this bill for FY1995–96, proposed and adopted in February 1995 by the Missouri House Appropriations Committee, was direct; it provided that "none of the expenditures from this appropriation for family planning activities shall go to any clinic which performs or actively promotes abortions as a method of family planning, and further provided that none of these funds may be used for administrative purposes at any clinic."

Over the next few months, the battle raged. As the appropriations bill moved from committee to committee, and from one house of the state legislature to the other, the limitation was first removed, then reinstated, and then removed again. When the issue reached the senate-house conference committee on April 25, 1995, the restriction was eliminated. But one week later, the house rejected the conference committee proposal, refusing to pass the appropriations bill for the Departments of Health and Mental Health, whereupon the conference committee relented and approved a provision meant to bar Planned Parenthood from access to family planning funding. Throughout, it was clear from the statements of legislators and reports in the press that the sole target of the limitation was Planned Parenthood. As the Republican house floor leader had predicted a month earlier in March, "If this is a game of chicken, I do not think the pro-life side is going to blink."[36]

The bill for FY1995–96, as passed, was similar to that which the house had initially passed and did not mention or refer to Planned Parenthood or abortion. It did not even include the prior years' restrictions on funding abortion directly (presumably because, as a practical matter, it applied only to Planned Parenthood, which would no longer be a grantee). Rather, it listed categories of authorized grantees, which, it was understood, did not include Planned Parenthood.

It is disturbing that there was, at best, minimal public discussion of the possible unconstitutionality of the statute. None of the many newspaper articles that I have read concerning the progress of the bill through the legislative process made any reference to the question of its constitutionality. Missouri publishes no legislative history or record of debates, so one cannot be certain what was discussed. However, the only reference to the issue during the debates of which there is a record is that a member of the Senate Appropriations Committee, Senator Harry Wiggins, stated to the committee that in his view it was not legal to exclude a specific provider of services from a state program and that it would be irresponsible for the Committee to adopt language doing so.[37] (In fact, the argument apparently was instrumental in having the restriction deleted prior to passage by the senate.)

The paucity of constitutional debate is particularly surprising, given the history of efforts to limit the availability of family planning funds for non-abortion-related services by Planned Parenthood and other abortion providers. Missouri was not the first; similar restrictions had been imposed by the Minnesota, Arizona, and the city of Wichita, Kansas. In each instance, the provision was challenged by a Planned Parenthood affiliate and was struck down by the federal courts. Indeed, the decision in the Minnesota case was summarily affirmed by the U.S. Supreme Court.[38] Rather, the debate in the Missouri legislature was on the wisdom of abortion and the practical effect on poor women of limiting funding. On the one side, there was the argument that the state should not support those who espouse an evil like abortion by funding any of their activities. On the other side, in addition to arguing that abortion was not evil, proponents asserted that the group really being punished was the indigent mothers seeking nonabortion family planning.

Missouri law provides for legal opinions to be given by the attorney general to the general assembly when requested.[39] It does not appear that the legal opinion of Attorney General Jay Nixon was sought or given. But abortion politics tend to be black and white, and it is unlikely that the antiabortion coalition would seek or trust a legal opinion given by an attorney general who, like Nixon, was considered prochoice.

In any event, in May 1996, Planned Parenthood of Mid-Missouri and Eastern Kansas, Inc., brought suit against the director of the Missouri Department of Health and other state officials seeking a declaratory judgment that the organization's exclusion from eligibility for state-appropriated family planning funds violated the Constitution. (Even before the legal challenge had commenced, however, the skirmishes within the legislature continued. In March 1996, antiabortion legislatures unsuccessfully attempted to delete all family planning funding after the governor refused to promise that no money would go to Planned Parenthood.[40]) In June 1996, Federal District Judge Fernando J. Gaitan Jr., issued a permanent injunction holding that Missouri could not exclude Planned Parenthood from participating in the family planning program, either because the organization provided abortions with its private funds or because it engaged in "public advocacy to protect safe and legal abortion services."[41] The injunction not only prohibited Planned Parenthood's exclusion as a service provider, it required the state to evaluate the organization's future proposal under criteria identical to those applied to all other participants.

The appropriations law for fiscal year 1996–97, passed prior to the decision, used the same language found in the FY1995–96 bill which had been challenged in the litigation before Judge Gaitan. When the judge rendered his decision in June 1996, the Planned Parenthood affiliates received reimbursement funding for the family planning services rendered during both FY1995–96 and FY1996–97. The issue of whether to appeal Judge Gaitan's ruling itself became a political issue. Both the governor and the attorney general were abortion rights supporters. Thus, while the attorney general had actively defended the funding restriction, it was assumed that both he and the governor were not displeased with the result.[42] Attorney General Jay Nixon did not appeal, leading to a new legislative fight over the FY1997–98 family planning appropriation.

As first introduced, the 1997–98 appropriations bill included no restrictions on the use of family planning funds, not even the restriction on their use for provision of abortions. At the same time, Missouri Right to Life was distributing a memo to all legislators, stating that the group "will be working hard to find a legal way to end state funding of abortionists, including Planned Parenthood. We look forward to working with legislators on the most appropriate way to address this problem." However, Missouri Right to Life recognized that the major impediment was not merely the state of the law in general, but rather the particular "final and binding" decision of the federal court addressed directly to the state.

> Based on the Court's ruling, it appears doubtful that any bill can provide for family planning grants to contractors that do not include Planned Parenthood, without violating the Court's injunction. It will not matter whether the provision is contained in an authorization bill or in an appropriation bill. Planned Parenthood has successfully portrayed itself in the eyes of a federal judge as a victim of nefarious, small-minded legislators, and the Court means to protect it from the General Assembly.[43]

The FY1997–98 bill was passed by the House Appropriations Committee and the House Budget Committee without change. Upon arrival on the floor of the house, it was met with a series of proposed amendments. The bill was passed by the house on April 1, 1997, with a provision that restricted the availability of family planning funds to public health agencies.

In the state senate, Senator Harry Wiggins, the same senator who had raised constitutional issues in vain in 1995, proposed an amendment that prohibited the use of family planning funds to support or subsidize abortions and provided for an independent audit to enforce the restriction. In his view such a provision was the limit that the legislature could go without running up against federal constitutional limitations. As thus modified, the bill passed the senate on April 9, 1997, causing the subject once again to be referred to a senate-house conference committee for resolution of the differences. The conference committee adopted the senate approach, but on May 8, 1997, was rebuffed by the house, continuing the stalemate. This stalemate over a violation of the federal constitution produced a violation of the Missouri Constitution. The state constitution requires that the budget and appropriation legislative process be completed by 6 P.M. of the first Friday following the first Monday in May; in 1997 the appointed day was May 9. Despite meetings of the House and the conference committee, no agreement was reached.

It was clear from statements made to the press that, despite the outstanding federal court decision and continuing injunction, the antiabortion bloc in the house was intent upon finding some way, without directly violating the court order, to prevent Planned Parenthood from receiving any funding. There was less concern about violating the Constitution. As described by the lobbyist for Campaign Life Missouri, the issue was "how to write a funding provision that would exclude only Planned Parenthood." Like the New York legislature when dealing with the issue of special education in Kiryas Joel, the attempt was to achieve the result previously held unconstitutional by drafting a statute that, on its face, cloaked its actual purpose.

On May 20, 1997, during a special session of the general assembly called, among other things, to consider and pass the still missing portions of the budget, the house passed a provision that its sponsor, Representative Gary Burton described "as constitutional as possible."[44] The complex provision can be likened to a multiple-choice test or a puzzle. It first stated that no payments could be made to organizations or affiliates of organizations that provide or promote abortions. This initial direction quite obviously violated the existing federal court order and the Constitution. The bill went on to provide that, if this provision was held invalid, it would have no effect and an alternative scheme would take effect pursuant to which only state and local governmental or quasi-government agencies would be eligible for funding, with the additional proviso that "none of these funds may be expended for the purpose of encouraging for[sic] abortion." Finally, the bill provided that if the alternative were held invalid, the funds would go solely to the state health department, and through it to city and county health departments. In part the legislative approach was that Planned Parenthood would be dissuaded from challenging the restriction out of compassion for its fellow not-for-profit private agencies that would be defunded by a finding of unconstitutionality. There is also a less obvious *sub rosa* text that would blame the federal court for the harm to women's health services caused by its 1996 finding of the unconstitutionality under the First Amendment of Planned Parenthood's exclusion as a service provider because of positions it had taken and statements it had made.

Some of the legislative debates on May 8, 9, and 22, 1997,

were disseminated on the Internet by the state, recorded by plaintiff's counsel, and then transcribed.[45] Although constitutional issues appeared in those transcripts from time to time, the recurrent theme of those seeking to defund Planned Parenthood was the need to effectuate the will of the people that state funds not be paid to a well-known abortion provider. To emphasize the connection to the public's will, the money was often referred to in the debates as "tax funds." An excellent illustration of the two points of view about the constitutional obligation of the legislature is found in the transcript of the debate in the house on May 22, 1997, just before it accepted the revised "multiple choice" version that had been originally proposed in the house:

> GENTLEMAN FROM DAVIESS: Mr. Speaker, where we are today, we stand on a day of history in the Missouri General Assembly that I think is a sad day in that what we are doing today is blatantly unconstitutional. I think every one knows and understands that. Now, it's not my intent to castigate a person on this floor. I respect every single person. And I respect every single person's ability to advance their position on an issue. But I also respect the constitution and I respect the process. And I think what we see here today for the second time [inaudible/feedback] when we cast all regard for the constitution to the wind in not making the final deadline, today we cast all respect for the constitution, we cast all respect for the legislative process and for the institution of the General Assembly to the wind, all to advance one [inaudible/feedback]. And Mr. Speaker, . . . regardless of the issue, regardless of a person's position on the issue, we should never allow ourselves to get to a point where we let any issue drive us to the position that we do not care, respect, and that we

do disregard what is so important to all of us as a process and the constitution that we are sworn to uphold. Mr. Speaker, I'm going to vote for the motion because we've got to have this bill. But Mr. Speaker, I think it is indeed a sad day in the history of the Missouri General Assembly.

To which a fellow House member responded:

GENTLEMAN FROM COLE: Mr. Speaker, all year long in the last four years I've set here and I just heard again a few minutes ago what I've heard for the last five years and that is, it's unconstitutional, it's unconstitutional, it's unconstitutional. I bet that's been said 2,000 times on this floor in the last five years. And what aggravates me about the process is, the gentleman just spoke said unconstitutional, he's not a member of the Supreme Court. That's what we have them over there for. They're the ones that's going to decide what's constitutional or not. What's important is, there's a 120 some people that voted in this body that listened to our constituents [feedback] and we're still in a democracy versus the other 20 on the other side, that's what's important, Mr. Speaker, that we do what is the will of the people that sent us here.[46]

Similarly, during the senate debate that resulted in the senate capitulating to the house version, State Senator Ted House said, "It's a matter of conscience. Let's do what we want to do; if it is ruled unconstitutional, we will deal with that." But State Senator Ken Jacob said, "The people in the House want us to pass a bill that is unconstitutional. It is just wrong, totally wrong."[47]

In these interplays, one discerns the core issue of what constitutes legislative responsibility, how one rationalizes voter mandate with the constitutional imperative. In this case the constitutional standard was clear; it had already been litigated and there was, even on the part of the legislators themselves, a general assumption that the revised bill would, at least at the trial court level, be held unconstitutional. But when, as here, the voter sentiment being followed by the legislature is religiously based, and when, as is likely the case here, the elected representatives have the same or similar religious views, there is a clash of values, religious and secular. When the religious view cannot under the Constitution be imposed involuntarily on those who do not choose to accept it, it is all the more important that the legislature and each legislator understand and accept the obligations imposed by the oath to uphold the Constitution.

On May 22, 1997, due to the unyielding posture of the antiabortion majority in the house and the practical human need to complete the budget, Missouri House Bill 20 passed the general assembly. Although Governor Carnahan disagreed with the bill and thought it unconstitutional, he signed it and promptly had a motion filed with Judge Gaitan to clarify whether and how the judge's prior order applied to the family planning funding provisions of the law. On June 30, 1997, after oral argument on the motion, the judge held that his prior order applied to the new law and found that all the restrictions violated both the spirit and the letter of the prior order.[48] The attorney general did not appeal. Ten legislators who had been supporters of the restrictions and were upset that the attorney general was not taking an appeal in an attempt to sustain the law they had passed sought to be permitted to intervene in the case so that they could appeal. Their application was denied both by Judge Gaitan and by the court of appeals.[49]

In 1998 the Missouri legislature again was preparing a budget, this time for the fiscal year 1998–99. Early in the year, the governor had introduced an appropriations bill, designated House Bill 1010. As in previous years, it included no limitations on who could receive family planning funds. On February. 11, 1998, at a meeting of the House Appropriations Committee, two amendments proposed by Representative David Reynolds were adopted. Together they struck the family planning provision of House Bill 1010, limited grantees to government agencies, and increased the appropriation by approximately thirteen million dollars to cover the additional cost of creating a governmental family planning infrastructure. When Reynolds was asked why he was creating a system that would cost more but provide reduced services, he replied that the antiabortionists had fought the fight for four years and had been stifled by the governor, the courts, and the attorney general. He suggested that this costly approach was the only "way to achieve our objective that is acceptable to the court." At one point during the debate one of the representatives said the extra millions were being spent because Planned Parenthood had not recognized the will of the people and withdrawn from the program. Although this approach was ultimately adopted by the house, because of its cost it was not accepted by the senate. Instead, the senate proposed passing a bill with language identical to that in the FY1997–1998 appropriation bill, which had been previously held unconstitutional by Judge Gaitan in his June 30, 1997, order. At the same time, the senate obtained a commitment from Attorney General Nixon that, if the prior year's language were repeated, Nixon would represent the Department of Health in an attack on the restrictions, and would appoint a special assistant attorney general designated by legislators to defend the appropriation's constitutionality. This allayed some of the concerns of the house majority that the restrictions had not been actively defended when they went before the court in 1997. On that basis the house concurred, and a statute that less than one year earlier had been held to violate a court order based on constitutional defects was passed again with the specific intent of seeking to overturn or circumvent the prior ruling.

Shortly after the FY1998–99 law was signed by the governor, Planned Parenthood and the attorney general separately filed papers in the federal court before Judge Gaitan seeking a ruling on the status of the bill in light of the court's prior order. Jordan B. Cherrick, who been had appointed special deputy attorney general to represent the interests of the legislature pursuant to Attorney General Nixon's commitment, filed in a state court, purportedly to obtain a state court interpretation of the meaning of the challenged provision and a ruling whether the restrictions were barred under the state constitution.[50] Since under the federal Constitution's Supremacy Clause the impact of a state constitution on a bill is irrelevant if the bill is unconstitutional under the federal Constitution, the purpose of the state filing was either misstated or to highlight the state/federal conflict. In any event, having paid approximately $90,000 for Planned Parenthood's counsel for the two previous court disputes, Missouri was now in the position of having to bear the cost of three sets of legal counsel in a probably futile effort to validate a statute already found constitutionally defective. On June 30, 1998, after some legal maneuvering that resulted in Cherrick participating in the federal proceeding, Judge Gaitan granted temporary relief to prevent the restrictions from taking effect on the grounds that they violated the Equal Protection Clause. The state (represented by Cherrick) appealed to the United States Court of Appeals for the Eighth Circuit. On February 3, 1999, that court issued a decision that both sides considered a victory.[51] The court found the statute to be ambiguous, read it to permit Planned Parenthood to receive family planning funds while at the same time engaging in abortion services through independent affiliates and, as thus interpreted, held the statute constitutional.

The judicial technique of interpreting an apparently unconstitutional statute in a way that brings it into the constitutional fold is not uncommon. While it is beneficial in that it does not require the legislature to start from scratch, with a period during which there is no applicable statute, there are harmful aspects as well. However, in such a case the legislature is rescued from its irresponsibility, reducing the incentive for the legislature to do its constitutional duty. In the spring of 1999, the Missouri legislature considered family planning funds for the fiscal year 1999–2000. Amplifying the ruling of the Eighth Circuit Court of Appeals and going beyond the Department of Health's initial guidelines, it passed a law providing that the groups seeking family planning money and their abortion affiliates must not share the same or even similar names. They cannot share medical facilities, business offices, or waiting rooms. Nor can they share expenses, employee wages, or equipment. The legislation also requires annual independent audits "to make sure Planned Parenthood complies with the rules."[52]

Conclusion

These two examples of repetitive unconstitutional legislation have many similarities and well as some notable differences. The core commonality is that both the Kiryas Joel and Missouri family planning disputes involved the repeated passage of unconstitutional legislation with a single purpose, in the former case to permit Kiryas Joel to set up a school district under circumstances that would not generally permit other communities to do so, and in the latter case to maintain a family planning program that excluded only Planned Parenthood from participation. In both cases the goals were religiously based, and both situations involved religious organizations lobbying to override core constitutional provisions. Finally, in both cases there was a significant political benefit to the legislators.

The politics of the two situations differed, however. Opposition to abortion had played a significant role in the campaigns and election of a number of the Missouri legislators and was a topic of concern to a significant number of Missouri voters. By contrast, there was no general popular interest in or concern about how the Satmar children in Kiryas Joel were to receive special education. Rather, the Hasidic Jewish communities in New York State themselves represented consolidated voting blocs that the political parties did not wish to offend. Both situations involved a substantial amount of posturing, but the New York example is more blatant because one doubts that most of the legislators who repeatedly voted for the school district were motivated by a strong belief in the substantive issue, while for some in the Missouri legislature such motivation is likely.

The harm in both cases is substantial. The legal cost to the states, both for their counsel and for the attorneys successfully challenging the statutes, was great. The diversion of staff, time, and attention of two not-for-profit organizations from their stated goals and purposes on a continuing and repeated basis deprived the public of other services. In Missouri, there was a repeated annual disruption of the budgetary and appropriation process. The most important harm of all, however, is the message that the Constitution and the oath of legislators to uphold it is superseded by strongly held views or major political benefits, which forces the courts—generally the federal courts—into ruling on these highly inflammatory political issues. Repetitive legislation declared unconstitutional by the courts places the judiciary in a position that undermines public respect for the courts and their rulings. As a general rule, the people of this nation look to the courts for resolution of public and private disputes and are willing to follow and abide by their decisions whether or not the people agree with them. Legislators must be willing to do so also, or have a reasonable and rational basis for challenging the courts' decisions in an appropriate manner. Further, when, as in these two examples, state legislation is at issue, the legislators put the federal courts in an adversary role with state government, raising states' rights issues in addition to legislative-judicial issues. This is often fostered, and taken advantage of, by state legislators, who adopt the excuse, "I tried to do right, but the meddling federal courts prevented me from doing so," which inappropriately promotes a disrespect for the law as expounded by the courts.

6

Legislative Reversal

In chapters 2, 3, and 4, I discussed examples of legislators passing laws that they know or have been advised to be unconstitutional and in chapter 5, I provided examples of legislatures repeatedly revising unconstitutional statutes in an attempt to mollify the courts by seeming to rectify the legislations' deficiencies. Yet another category in the continuing tension between legislative expression of political and popular desires, on the one hand, and judicial maintenance of constitutional limitations, on the other, is the attempt of legislatures to reverse unpopular Supreme Court interpretations of the Constitution.

Such reversals can be divided into two types. The first involves rewriting the statute that was annulled or limited, or drafting a different statute, to achieve the desired end while avoiding the constitutional problem. As early as 1793, Congress took such a step when it amended the statute after the Court had invalidated a pension law in *Hayburn's Case*.[1] This approach is an appropriate one. When, however, the legislature, rather than curing the constitutional defect, tries to obfuscate it, one gets a situation like the Kiryas Joel School Board statutes and cases discussed in chapter 5.

In the second group are cases where the unpopularity of the decision derives from the substance of the interpretation given to the constitutional provision itself. The appropriate remedy for such a situation is to amend the constitutional provision. For example, when the Supreme Court held that a citizen of one state could sue another state in the federal courts,[2] Congress and states passed the Eleventh Amendment to reverse the result. A constitutional amendment is not easily enacted, however; nor, in the view of many members of Congress and others, should it be lightly sought. Thus, from time to time Congress attempts to eliminate constitutional impediment by a simple statute.

I shall examine two such attempts, the first involving an accused's rights to counsel and against self-incrimination and the second involving the First Amendment right of free exercise of religion and prohibition on the establishment of religion. Both of these—crime and religion—are issues of high emotional and political content.

Attempts to reverse Court decisions draw on two concurrent strains of thought. One is a popular dissatisfaction with a particular Supreme Court decision, often coupled with one or more organized groups interested in actively taking up the cudgels in support of a legislative reversal. This is often supported by reference to the second strain, that the original intent of the constitutional founders was more limited than recognized by the Court, and that this intent has been subverted by the federal bureaucracy and an "activist Court."[3]

Congressional attempts to reverse Supreme Court constitutional decisions raise different issues than were raised by the reckless passage of unconstitutional laws discussed in the earlier chapters. When a legislature passes an unconstitutional law, either once or repetitively, it often does so without adequate fact-finding or constitutional inquiry, shifting the burden of protecting constitutional rights and values to the courts and those who feel strongly enough about such values and rights to commence litigation.

Most congressional attempts to overturn a Supreme Court constitutional decision by statute desire to loosen or eliminate a restriction imposed by a constitutionally granted right, particularly in the criminal law area. The attempt to reverse the *Miranda* decision discussed later in this chapter is such an attempt. Such statutory attempts at reversal raise constitutional issues at two levels: first, whether the substantive law change contained in the statute is constitutionally permissible and, second, even if it is permissible, whether Congress has the power to declare and effectuate the change under our federal system.[4]

Congressional dissatisfaction derived from what is perceived by Congress as the Court's failure sufficiently to extend the scope of a constitutional right is a far less common occurrence. In such a case, as with the Religious Freedom Restoration Act (RFRA), Congress is granting rights or imposing limitations that the courts have found to be not required by the Constitution; therefore the only constitutional issued raised is that of congressional power within a federal system.

Miranda and the Omnibus Crime Control Act

Since the passage of the Fourteenth, Fifteenth, and Sixteenth Amendments to the Constitution (the Civil War amendments), the concept of equality has been a hallmark of constitutional thought. In the landmark 1966 decision of *Miranda v. Arizona*,[5] the Supreme Court set down broad rules to ensure that the privilege against self-incrimination would be equally available to the well-informed and the uninformed, to the educated and the uneducated. In that case, the Court held that a defendant's statement resulting from police interrogation could not be used against the defendant unless the defendant had been advised of his right to remain silent, of the fact that any statement could be used against him, and of his right to have an attorney present, either retained or provided by the state. The decision, which was decided by the narrow margin of 5-4, did not establish or broaden the constitutional right against self-incrimination or right to counsel; rather it established a rule that prevented the inadvertent or unknowing loss or waiver of those rights.

The decision was praised in some circles and condemned in others. (Interestingly, despite the vehemence of the condemnations and the predictions that the requirement would materially hamper law enforcement, the *Miranda* warning had been prescribed FBI practice prior to the decision.) Congress and law enforcement groups were in the condemnatory group. As Senator Sam J. Ervin (D-NC), a former justice of the North Carolina Supreme Court, expressed it: "[T]here is no question that these decisions [*Miranda*, *Mallory v. U.S.* (arraignment may not be unnecessarily delayed) and *U.S. v. Wade* (right to counsel at police lineups)] have resulted in the freeing of multitudes of criminals of undoubted guilt and have unduly hampered legitimate law enforcement activities. The situation must be rectified and the duty to do so devolves rightly upon the Congress."[6] This statement, apparently disregarding the constitutional issue of legislative power, reflects the emotion of the time related to the issue of crime. Congress, avowedly motivated by a "fear" of "lawlessness," the rampant scourge of "organized crime," and engaged in a "war" against the criminal element of the citizenry, was intent on passing a law was designed to supersede *Miranda* and certain other decisions of the Warren Court.

This law, entitled the Omnibus Crime Control and Safe Streets Act of 1968, was a reaction to the "ghetto riots of 1964, 1965, 1966, 1967 and 1968 [in the Watts section of Los Angeles, Newark, Detroit and Washington, D.C.] which [Congress believes] represent crime in its most aggravated form."[7] Finding such riots to be the equivalent of "war,"[8] Congress first proposed to provide monetary aid to the states to meet the threat. But then, turning to *Miranda* and its sister cases, the Senate Judiciary Committee saw yet another need:

> No matter how much money is spent for upgrading police departments, for modern equipment, for research and other purposes encompassed in title I, crime will not be effectively abated so long as criminals who have voluntarily confessed their crimes are released on mere technicalities. The traditional right of the people to have their prosecuting attorneys place in evidence before juries the voluntary confessions and incriminating statements made by defendants simply must be restored.

This view ultimately prevailed, and Title II, initially proposed in the Senate by Senators McClellan (D-Ark) and Ervin (D-NC), became part of the Omnibus Crime Control and Safe Streets Act of 1968.

On the issue of the application of the *Miranda* rule to the admissibility of confessions, the Act added § 3501, which provided that, in a federal case, a confession "shall be admissible in evidence if it is voluntarily given." It then also provided that the determination of voluntariness shall be based on the consideration of five factors: the time between arrest and arraignment, if the confession was made before arraignment; whether the defendant knew the nature of the offense of which he was suspected; whether the defendant had been advised of his right against self-incrimination; whether the defendant had been advised of his right to the assistance of counsel; and whether the defendant had counsel when he was questioned and confessed. The section concludes by stating that the "presence or absence of any of the . . . factors to be taken into consideration by the judge need not be conclusive on the issue of voluntariness of the confession." Under the statute, rather than the giving of the *Miranda* warning being mandatory, it would become one of five factors in a balancing test.

This was certainly not a case where legislators doubted what the constitutional standard was, and what the Supreme Court had said. Congress and most of those testifying, particularly from the law enforcement community, knew all too well what *Miranda* held. Rather, as we will see with RFRA and the *Smith* decision, it was simply that Congress thought the decision was wrong and harmful. The debate was highly confrontational, featuring regular attacks on the *Miranda* decision, and on the Court and the five justices in the majority.

The question of congressional power was therefore discussed at length, and with varying degrees of sophistication. At one extreme were those who saw it as an issue of pure power and made arguments echoing the tripartite theory of coequal power of each of the three branches of government. Representative (and later president) Gerald Ford (R-MI), who was the minority leader of the House, took a more extreme view, suggesting legislative supremacy: "I refuse to concede . . . that the elected representatives of the American people cannot be the winner in a confrontation with the U.S. Supreme Court. To admit that is to admit that the American people cannot control the U.S. Supreme Court."[9] A more sophisticated argument was that since, as the Supreme Court subsequently described it,[10] the *Miranda* rule was a prophylactic standard, it was not constitutionally required. However, as Charles Alan Wright of the University of Texas Law School has pointed out, it is one thing to provide alternative standards and quite another to provide, as § 3501 does, that no safeguards are needed.[11] Senators Wayne Morse (D-OR) and Joseph Tydings (D-MD), as well as Representative Emanuel Celler (D-NY), the chair of the House Judiciary Committee, were of the view that reversing *Miranda* required a constitutional amendment.[12] Tydings, who was the floor manager for those who opposed Title II in the Senate, submitted 212 letters from legal scholars, 43 letters from law schools, and 24 letters from law deans supporting his view. But none of this impressive array had the opportunity to testify, a fact that Senator Tydings complained of and that was attributed by commentators to the fact that Senator McClellan as chair "held firm control over the schedule of witnesses."[13] Statements of opposition were also submitted by the Judicial Conference of the United States (the conference of the federal judiciary) and the Criminal Law Section of the American Bar Association. President Johnson, although he ultimately signed the bill into law, urged Senator Mansfield not to encumber the other beneficial parts of the law "with provisions raising grave constitutional questions."[14]

The Senate Judiciary Committee report hedged its bets, first claiming constitutionality and then predicting that, in any event, by the time the case got to the Supreme Court, *Miranda* would not be upheld, either because of greater wisdom or a change in the composition of the Court:

> The committee is aware that a few have expressed the view that legislation by Congress restoring the voluntariness test to the admissibility of confessions and

incriminating statements would be declared unconstitutional, on the ground that the provisions do not measure up to the rigid standards set forth in the majority opinion in *Miranda*. The committee, however, is aware also that the overwhelming weight of the testimony adduced by the subcommittee supported the passage of these provisions of the bill, and that the vast majority of the witnesses expressed no doubt as to the constitutionality of the legislation. The Committee is also aware that the opinions of the four dissenting Justices clearly indicate that neither[sic] of them would consider these provisions unconstitutional. . . .

The committee feels that it is obvious from the opinion of Justice Harlan and other dissenting Justices . . . that the overwhelming weight of judicial opinion in this country is that the voluntariness test does not offend the Constitution or deprive a defendant of any constitutional right. No one can predict with assurance what the Supreme Court might at some future date decide if these provisions are enacted. The committee has concluded that this approach to the balancing of the rights of society and the rights of the individual served us well over the years, that it is constitutional and that Congress should adopt it. After all, the *Miranda* decision itself was by a bare majority of one, and with increasing frequency the Supreme Court has reversed itself. The committee feels that by the time the issue of constitutionality would reach the Supreme Court, the probability is that this legislation would be upheld.[15]

This statement is a rejection of the "judicial monopoly" approach of constitutional interpretation. The report first cites the testimony that suggested that the *Miranda* decision did not really require *Miranda* warnings; those were just one way to achieve the constitutionally mandated result. It then suggests that the Supreme Court is unreliable, particularly when the controlling precedent was adopted by a narrow margin, and appears to conclude with the expectation that the Supreme Court will follow the lead of Congress and recognize its prior error.

By June 1968, the bill, including § 3501, became law. The process of adopting § 3501 illustrates a number of the problems that arise when serious constitutional questions are raised concerning a politically popular bill. Often, as here, the popularity of the proposal is so strong that no politically viable substantive response to the proposal is possible. That is compounded when the unconstitutionality relates to bills involving criminal justice and procedures. In such cases, the persons whose interests are most affected are those who have been accused of crime and those who may be accused in the future. The former are unlikely to offer to testify and, in any event, would not carry much political weight; the latter do not yet know they are in the category. The debate then becomes one between the proponents of the bill on the one hand, who put forward the many benefits of the proposal, and the opponents of the bill on the other hand, who cite the constitutional infirmities of the proposal. The arguments pass one another like ships in the night. Such a debate encourages concepts of balancing the substantive need or benefits against the constitutional "harm," as is fact suggested in the excerpt from the Senate committee report quoted earlier. It also leads to legislators considering constitutional arguments as "merely" a device used to oppose legislation about which substantive objections cannot be raised without causing political harm to the objector. Constitutional arguments are used by some legislators in such a manner for such purposes. However, such a contention should not be used by legislators to dismiss constitutional concerns out of hand unless they have considered the constitutional issue and found it frivolous.

One aspect of legislative recklessness is the irresponsible use of the hearing process. One of the strengths of the legislative process (and a necessary element in passing rational legislation) is a legislature's ability to find facts and expose opposing views to the light of scrutiny. Judge J. Edward Lumbard, then chief judge of the U.S. Court of Appeals for the Second Circuit, had testified before the Senate Judiciary Committee subcommittee on the bill, addressing Congress's failure to establish laws and rules in this area, forcing courts to establish rules without benefit of the legislative fact-finding process. In his testimony he described the benefits of the legislative process:

> The legislative process permits a wide variety of views to be screened and testimony can be taken from those who know the facts.
>
> The legislative process is far better calculated to set standards and rules by statute than is the process of announcing principles through court decision in particular cases where the facts are limited. The legislative process is better adapted to seeing the situation in all its aspects and establishing a system and rules which can govern a multitude of different cases.
>
> Judges seldom have before them all those who are best informed regarding practical problems and the difficulties in living with any proposed change in the law.[16]

Judge Lumbard obviously assumed that the legislature would approach its fact-finding and opinion-finding role seriously and fairly. But as we have seen with the legislative process leading up to the passage of laws regulating Internet content by Congress, by the New York legislature, and by the New

Mexico legislature, laws are sometimes enacted with few if any legislative hearings and little or no other serious fact-finding. It is equally a dereliction of legislative duty to slant the hearings by excluding spokespersons for one or more points of view. Such an exclusion has the potential of misleading other members of the legislature and changes what should be a fact-finding process to the creation of a supportive record for a preordained result. The Senate hearings concerning § 3501 were one-sided, reflecting Senator McClellan's desire for passage. The fact that single-focus hearings do occur despite the best efforts of those who oppose a proposal to appear and be heard makes it less surprising when courts fail to give legislative choices the deference to which they might otherwise be entitled.

The postpassage history of § 3501 is also interesting. There has been no constitutional confrontation between Congress and the Supreme Court since, for the most part, the statute has been disregarded.[17] In many respects, this fact is puzzling. It should not be surprising that President Johnson, who had early qualms about the provision's constitutionality, continued the FBI practice of giving the warning and that Attorney General Ramsey Clark directed that the Justice Department would only offer into evidence confessions that complied with *Miranda*.[18] The subsequent history under Presidents Nixon, Reagan, and Bush *is* surprising.

At the time of the hearings, Richard M. Nixon was campaigning for the Republican Party nomination for the presidency. On May 9, 1968, he issued his position paper on crime. It attacked the Supreme Court for the *Miranda* decision and urged "Congress to enact proposed legislation that—dealing with both *Miranda* and *Escobedo*—would leave it to the judge and jury to determine both the voluntariness and the validity of any confession."[19] The paper specifically stated support for Title II. In January 1969, after the passage of § 3501,

Nixon was sworn in as president. His first attorney general, John Mitchell, directed Justice Department employees to comply with *Miranda*, but permitted recourse to § 3501 in borderline cases when "a voluntary confession is obtained after a less than perfect warning or a less than perfect waiver."[20] For the most part the issue did not reach the courts; the only court of appeals decision held that the trial court was correct in applying § 3501 but then went on to find that, in any event, there had been full compliance with *Miranda*, making the earlier statement extraneous.[21] This practice continued through the Reagan administration, as Attorney General Edward Meese, one of the most outspoken critics of the *Miranda* ruling, did not actively promote use of the statute. Presently, the Clinton administration has taken the position that it will not rely on § 3501, even when specifically questioned by the Supreme Court and other courts.[22]

One recent tactic used by conservative groups who desire to establish the constitutionality of § 3501 so that it will become operative is to seek appropriate cases with sympathetic judges and then to apply for permission to join the case as an amicus curiae (friend of the court) to argue for the application of § 3501.[23] Two recent opinions directly finding the section constitutional arises out of such a situation. The first, in 1997 by a federal trial court, was decided after the defendant had fled, and therefore matters are held in abeyance until he is apprehended and available.[24] Thus, the case and the decision, unlike the defendant, are going nowhere.

The second case involves an appeal from a federal trial court that suppressed a confession because of a failure to give the notice of rights required by *Miranda*. The Court of Appeals for the Fourth Circuit (covering Maryland, Virginia, West Virginia, North Carolina, and South Carolina), as urged by an amicus brief by Professor Paul Cassell, for years a crusader against the *Miranda* rule, held by a vote of 2-1 that it would apply § 3501 to reverse the trial court. The Fourth Circuit acted even though the government prosecutors had not made any argument based on § 3501.[25] As the majority stated, "[T]he Department of Justice cannot prevent us from deciding this case under the governing law simply by refusing to argue it." (One can certainly characterize this as judicial activism from the right.) The majority cavalierly dismissed the constitutional objections to § 3501, relying in part on the one-sided hearings, which the court described as "utilizing . . . [Congress's] superior fact-finding ability." The dissenting judge, highlighting the fact that neither party had raised, or argued for or against the applicability or constitutionality of § 3501, strongly argued that it was inappropriate for the court to consider the issue. Defense counsel requested reconsideration by all the judges of the Fourth Circuit Court of Appeals, which was denied by a vote of 8-5. At the time this is being written, Supreme Court review of the decision is being sought. Thus, at this time, § 3501 has been in the statute books for twenty years, and neither its constitutionality nor its efficacy has been seriously tested.

Religious Freedom Restoration Act

The Religious Freedom Restoration Act (which came to be known as RFRA) is another clear example of a legislative attempt to reverse the Supreme Court. The legislative history is replete with broad and specific statements of that intention. In 1990, a bipartisan coalition led by Representative Steven Solarz (D-NY) introduced RFRA as a bill that was expressly designed to correct the perceived shortcomings and the probable consequences of a decision of the United States

Supreme Court, *Oregon Employment Division v. Smith*.[26] Three years later, it passed both houses with relative ease and sizable majorities (ninety-seven senators voted in favor of the bill). President Clinton signed it into law with some fanfare on January 5, 1994. Yet, another three years later, in *City of Boerne v. Flores*,[27] the Supreme Court struck down RFRA (at least to the extent that it limited state and local, rather than federal, action), holding that the Fourteenth Amendment does not grant Congress "substantive" powers, but rather only "remedial" power to redress violations of rights as established by the Court. Citing *Marbury v. Madison*, Justice Kennedy emphasized the Court's authority "to say what the law is."[28]

After the decision, supporters of RFRA, both in Congress and elsewhere, vowed to overturn the ruling by constitutional amendment or by the states passing "little RFRA's."[29] A number of states, including Alabama, Florida, and Illinois, have already passed RFRA-equivalents, which do not raise the federalism and congressional-power questions that caused the demise of federal RFRA. In 1998, a new bill, called the Religious Liberty Protection Act (called "son of RFRA" by its opponents), was pushed in Congress, yet another example of the "if at first you don't succeed, try again" approach discussed in chapter 5.[30]

Before examining in detail the legislative process that resulted in the passage of RFRA, an irony is worth noting. RFRA is a statute that limits the power of federal, state, and local legislatures to pass general laws applying to religious institutions or impinging on religious rights. Thus, in both the *Smith* and *City of Boerne* decisions, the Supreme Court expanded legislative power at the expense of the First Amendment. This is certainly not, as some say of *Miranda*, an example of an "activist" judiciary expanding constitutional restrictions. While the *Smith*/RFRA debate may appear to reverse the usual roles and positions of the Court and Congress, the debate can also be viewed as relating to political power—which branch has the right to set the scales of the balance of power. On a more practical level, the position taken by Congress in enacting RFRA may simply reflect the political power of the broad range of religious groups urging the passage of RFRA.

The underlying substantive issue arose on April 15, 1990, when the United States Supreme Court decided *Oregon Employment Division v. Smith*.[31] In that case two men, Smith and Black, were fired from a drug rehabilitation agency because they had ingested peyote, a hallucinogenic drug, for sacramental purposes at a Native American Church. Oregon state law prevented the payment of unemployment compensation to persons who had been fired for job-related misconduct. The use of peyote violated state criminal laws that did not have an exemption for drug use for religious purposes. Prior Supreme Court precedents had required the federal government or a state to demonstrate a "compelling governmental interest" to permit the application of a general statute in a way that impacted on religious activities.[32] The *Smith* Court, by a vote of 6-3, held that a law of general application that was not specifically intended to restrict religious practice and did not establish any particular religious practice could be enforced in accordance with its terms even though, as in *Smith,* it would have the effect of punishing someone for the exercise of his or her religious practices or beliefs.

One would think it unlikely that Congress would object to a decision that gave it and state legislatures greater license to exercise legislative power and discretion freely. To the contrary, however, representatives and senators berated the decision. In great part this was because of the creation of an ecumenical coalition ultimately consisting, among others, of Baptists, Jews (both traditional and liberal), Muslims,

Buddhists, Quakers, Evangelicals, and Presbyterians, as well as the ACLU, People for the American Way, Americans United for the Separation of Church and State, and the Traditional Values Coalition, which lobbied for a change in the decision. Even at the earliest stages, however, press reports of the uproar mentioned possible constitutional impediments to a legislative reversal of the *Smith* rule.[33]

Reflecting the strong opposition to, and concern about, the *Smith* decision, legislation was introduced very early in the next congressional session. On July 26, 1990, only a few months after the decision, the Religious Freedom Restoration Act of 1990 was filed in the House. In line with the combative title that it had been given, the legislation did not attempt to disguise its motivation. The bill stated:

> in *Employment Division v. Smith* . . . the Supreme Court virtually eliminated the requirement that the government justify burdens on religious exercise imposed by laws neutral toward religion.[34]

Its stated purposes were equally unambiguous:

> to restore the compelling interest test as set forth in *Sherbert v. Verner* . . . and *Wisconsin v. Yoder* . . . and to guarantee its application in all cases where free exercise of religion is substantially burdened.[35]

In effect, RFRA was throwing down a gauntlet before the Supreme Court. By naming *Smith* in the body of the bill itself, the congressional sponsors were both acknowledging the Court's decision and declaring the decision to be wrong and unjust. By its terms, RFRA suggested that Congress was the ultimate arbiter of constitutional interpretation.

When the initial hearings of the Subcommittee on Civil and Constitutional Rights of the House Judiciary Committee were held on September 27, 1990, virtually all of the testimony related to the error of *Smith* and the probably untoward consequences of that decision. However, Representative William E. Dannemayer, a Republican who was one of the sponsors of the bill, recognized that RFRA "was not your normal piece of reasoned jurisprudence." He continued:

> Congress is the voice of the people, and while the legislative branch is not in the business of determining what is constitutional and what is not, we are entrusted as a check and balance to the judicial branch. Perhaps this exercise will remind the "religion last" crowd of the danger of legislating by judiciary.[36]

This is a militant statement of the tripartite approach to the determination of the meaning of the Constitution, which had been soundly rejected by Chief Justice Marshall in *Marbury v. Madison* 150 years earlier. It reflects, in part, the emotional undercurrents that are present when a decision affects a broad range of religions and religionists.

Representative Steven Solarz, the primary sponsor of RFRA, suggested a more modest route to constitutionality: "This legislation restores the religious rights of all Americans as they were prior to *Smith* without tampering with the Bill of Rights. Rather, . . . [it]would simply create a statutory right consistent with the Congress' powers under section five of the fourteenth amendment."[37]

In an exchange before the subcommittee, Dannemayer took up the issue with Solarz. "This citizen in America happens to believe that there are products of our Supreme Court going back . . . to 1962 which should be reversed. . . . Would you support that?" Solarz responded, "If we can assemble the same coalition in support of your proposal . . . I would certainly be prepared to consider it." At this point Edwards chimed in, "How about throwing in *Roe v. Wade?*" Solarz replied, "If we're really going to go after all of the

Supreme Court decisions using this bill as a vehicle . . . you might want to consider *Baker v. Carr* . . . as well."[38]

This exchange is puzzling. Representative Solarz's comment reflects an understanding of the difference between constitutional rights and statutory rights, as well as the fact that the issue raised by RFRA is not substantive constitutionality but rather congressional power. A reversal of *Roe v. Wade* (dealing with abortion rights) or *Baker v. Carr* (one person, one vote), on the other hand, would constitute a limitation of substantive constitutional rights found to exist by the Supreme Court, a very different matter. The colloquy may well have had a whimsical or sarcastic tone not reflected in the transcript. It does suggest, however, that once Congress is in the business of reviewing Supreme Court decisions, anything can happen.

The only direct discussion of Congress's constitutional power at this first hearing came when Representative Edwards asked, "Do any of the witnesses have a problem with Congress' right to enact this legislation? . . . Do you think that down the road the Court might say that Congress doesn't have this right?"[39] In response, Edwards was directed by the Reverend Dean Kelley, director of Religious Liberty of the National Council of Churches, to a letter that had been submitted to the subcommittee by Professor Douglas Laycock of the University of Texas School of Law (who subsequently argued the case in support of the constitutionality of RFRA in the Supreme Court on behalf of the Roman Catholic Archdiocese of San Antonio), arguing that Congress was empowered to pass RFRA under Section 5 of the Fourteenth Amendment.[40]

At a subsequent subcommittee meeting on May 13, 1992, Representative Henry Hyde (R-IL) again raised the issue. He did not mince words:

First, this is an exercise in incompetence. We lack the legal competence to override a Supreme Court interpretation of the Constitution. Congress is institutionally unable to restore a prior interpretation of the first amendment once the Supreme Court has rejected that interpretation. We are a legislature, not a court. . . . Are we able to . . . tell the Court, "You guys follow *Sherbert* and *Yoder*, not these other seventy-five cases?" Is that a little arrogant . . . on the part of the legislative branch?

Hyde then had a dialogue with Professor Nadine Strossen, the president of the ACLU, who contended that Congress had not only the power but the responsibility to protect civil liberties "when the Court has failed to do so." Hyde was not convinced. At the next day's hearing, written statements on the issues of congressional power and constitutionality were submitted by Professor Edward Gaffney of Valparaiso Law School in support of the appropriateness of RFRA, and Professor Ira Lupu of Cornell Law School opposing RFRA, the latter responded to by Professor Laycock. Thus, in the 1992 House subcommittee hearings there was a fairly extensive discussion of the issue of federalism and congressional power.

House subcommittee hearings were held in 1992, and there was a major push by supporters of RFRA to move and pass the bill before the 1992 elections. Despite the strength and breadth of the initial support for RFRA, however, RFRA remained bottled up. Some of the delay may be attributable to constitutional concerns, although the preponderance of the testimony suggested that Congress did not consider them weighty. In addition to Professor Laycock, who was a reputable scholar, Floyd Abrams, one of the nation's leading

First Amendment scholars, argued that Congress had the power to overrule Supreme Court First Amendment decisions to the extent of expanding the penumbra of First Amendment protection.[41] In addition, in February 1991 the American Bar Association House of Delegates urged the passage of RFRA; it followed this with a letter of support to House subcommittee chair Don Edwards, dated June 23, 1992, when the debate was heating up. Other than Professor Lupu, who had made an earlier statement, only Bruce Fein, a conservative who had been general counsel of the FCC during the Reagan administration, forcefully and publicly argued that the bill was unconstitutional, both in articles and in testimony before Congress.[42] A second concern raised by some was the belief that prisoners would raise hundreds, if not thousands, of claims under RFRA, were it passed.

Clearly, the major impediment to passage was the highly active opposition of the United States Catholic Conference and the National Right to Life Committee during this two-year period. Only when this opposition relented did RFRA pass. These organizations feared that Jewish women might successfully use RFRA to challenge bans on abortion, since Talmudic law states that abortion is not a choice but a religious duty when the life of the mother is threatened. While many supporters of the bill found this concern unwarranted, the lobbying on behalf of the conference was intense, and its opposition was effective during this period. (It is interesting that throughout the three-year legislative history of RFRA, it was strongly supported by Christian fundamentalist churches which, like the Catholic Conference, also support the antiabortion right-to-life position.)

As early as February 1991, the National Right to Life Committee had sent a letter to Congress stating that it would oppose RFRA unless the bill excepted religious rights relating to abortions. In the fall of 1991, Representative

Robert Dornan (R-CA) signed on to the bill, only to withdraw after lobbying pressure. And Senator Joseph Biden (D-DE), who was to cosponsor the Senate version of RFRA with Senator Orrin Hatch (R-UT), eventually decided not to participate in such a visible way. Early in 1992, Representative Christopher Smith (R-NJ) filed a bill that was similar to RFRA but included an abortion exception. Throughout, President George Bush waffled on the issue, never supporting RFRA and at times appearing to oppose it, a position generally assumed to reflect his desire not to offend Catholic antiabortion groups.

Early in 1993, RFRA was once again introduced in the House, by Congressman Charles Schumer and in the Senate by Senators Orrin Hatch and Edward Kennedy (D-MA). This began a push that, with the active support of recently elected President Bill Clinton and his administration, and with the disappearance of Catholic Conference opposition, would result within a year in passage and signing by the president. There was extensive debate and discussion in 1993 both in committee and on the floor. Very little of it related to the issue of constitutionality, which for the most part appeared by then to be a nonissue. Since Professor Douglas Laycock, leading First Amendment lawyer Floyd Abrams, the American Bar Association, and Attorney General Janet Reno, who had submitted a letter in support of RFRA, all saw no problem, why should Congress be concerned? Thus there was relatively little debate on the issue of constitutionality in 1993. The only direct public discussion in Congress of RFRA's constitutionality during 1993 took place on the Senate floor on October 27, 1993. Senator Charles Grassley (R-IA), after stating his intent to support the bill, said:

> I should note that I have had some reservations about the bill. Congress must tread very carefully when

legislating standards for the freedom of religion. When we considered the bill in the Judiciary Committee, I raised concerns about Congress' constitutional authority to enact legislation dictating to the Supreme Court what standards it must employ in free exercise cases, and about the wisdom of mandating a compelling interest standard in all cases. Fortunately the Senator from Utah [Hatch] was able to alleviate many of these objections.[43]

Grassley then requested that his colloquy with Hatch be printed in the *Congressional Record*. While much of it relates to other issues, such as the effect of RFRA on prison regulation and the military, it begins:

> Mr. Grassley: What is the basis for congressional power to enact this bill? Do we have the authority to prescribe a specific standard for the Supreme Court?
>
> Mr. Hatch: In my view there is constitutional authority to defend the first amendment's protection of our religious freedom. Congress has the power to regulate state action under section 5 of the 14th amendment to the Constitution. The due process clause of the 14th amendment provides that authority and it has consistently been held to incorporate and apply the first amendment to the states. Constitutional scholars, including professor Douglas Laycock of the University of Texas, have testified before our committee to this effect.[44]

From the perspective of a member of Congress, passage of RFRA can readily be considered as authorized, or even compelled, by the member's constitutional oath, rather than in derogation of that oath. As Nadine Strossen, the president of the ACLU, bluntly put it when she testified in support of

RFRA: "All of you take an oath to uphold and defend the Constitution, and it is particularly important that you do so in a situation such as this when . . . the Supreme Court . . . has failed to do so." Or, as a member of Congress phrased it at one of the subcommittee hearings, "As a Congressman you have a duty to uphold the Constitution. You certainly don't want to defer to the Supreme Court as to your constitutional duty." The *Smith* case was characterized by members as "diminishing religious liberty," "transforming a most hallowed liberty into a mundane concept with little more status than a fishing license," "unfortunate," "virtually eliminating the first amendment's protection of the free exercise of religion," and a "devastating blow to" and "serious erosion of" First Amendment rights. Thus Congress saw itself in the posture of reaffirming prior First Amendment jurisprudence against an unwarranted attack by the judiciary, by taking a position that garnered the appreciation of most organized religious groups, although it was never clear how broad the interest was among the general population, even those with religious ties.

When RFRA was passed, it did not face a court challenge mounted by its opponents. Interestingly enough, the "usual suspects"—the civil liberties organizations that are often in the forefront of constitutional challenges—were in this instance mostly part of the coalition that had fought *for* RFRA for three years, reflecting again the view that RFRA was necessary to redeem First Amendment liberties. Instead, the challenge that ended up in the Supreme Court arose out of the growth of the congregation at St. Peter Catholic Church in Boerne, Texas, a city near San Antonio. The city had recently established a historic landmark commission. When the local archbishop filed for a building permit to enlarge the church, the permit was denied as incompatible with the neighborhood historic district. Archbishop Flores sued in the federal court, challenging the denial for, among other reasons, violation of RFRA. The trial court held RFRA to be unconstitutional as it exceeded the scope of congressional power under § 5 of the Fourteenth Amendment, the major rationale discussed in the congressional hearings.[45] The court of appeals reversed, finding RFRA to be constitutional, which brought the case to the Supreme Court.[46]

As had the trial court, the Supreme Court held RFRA unconstitutional on the ground that Congress had exceeded its constitutional powers.[47] The opinion of the Court, written by Justice Kennedy, at the outset dwelt on the fact the Congress had debated the points of constitutional interpretation found in *Smith,* criticized the Court's reasoning, and had stated as its purpose to restore the law as it had been before *Smith.* The Court, quoting from *Marbury v. Madison,* pointed out that courts determine the constitutionality of laws and that the power of Congress is limited by the Constitution. The Court found that the purpose of RFRA was "to attempt a substantive change in constitutional protections," but that the "design of the [Fourteenth] Amendment and the text of § 5 are inconsistent with the suggestion that Congress has the power to decree the substance of the Fourteenth Amendment's restrictions on the States."[48] Not even the three dissenters argued that RFRA fell within the power given to Congress in § 5 to enforce the provisions of the Fourteenth Amendment; rather they would have reconsidered and reversed *Smith* and then reviewed RFRA to determine whether it was consistent with the pre-*Smith* law.[49]

Congress probably had and has the power to limit its own legislative power by subjecting it to the strictures of RFRA, and the cases since *Boerne* have so held.[50] Nor is there a real question—subject to issues that may arise under state constitutions—that state legislatures may pass state laws like RFRA which apply to state agencies, and a number of states, including Alabama, Florida, and Illinois, have done so. Senators Hatch and Kennedy and Representatives Canady and Nadler, leading supporters in Congress of RFRA, filed the Religious Liberty Protection Act (RLPA), and the first hearing was held in July 1998. In an attempt to solve the issue of congressional power that caused the demise of RFRA, RLPA attempts to gain legitimacy by applying only to programs or activities operated by a government that received federal financial assistance, or to matters in or affecting interstate commerce. At the time this is being written, the prospects for passage of the revised bill are uncertain. Similarly, even if passed, it is not clear how the law will be considered by the courts.

A comparison of the motivations behind the enactment of RFRA and § 3501 reveals both similarities and differences. Both reflected an almost nostalgic desire to return to the rule as it had been. Both were fueled by vocal, politically adept citizen groups. The goals to be achieved, on the other hand, were diametrically opposite. The objection to *Miranda* was that the Supreme Court had unduly expanded the individual rights protected by the Constitution; Congress sought to limit those rights. With RFRA, it was just the opposite, a much more unusual scenario. The objection was that the Supreme Court had insufficiently protected the First Amendment right to free expression of religion; Congress sought to expand those rights.

Congress acted irresponsibly in relation to both Title II of the Omnibus Crime Control Act and the RFRA. With respect to the former, the hearings, while extensive, virtually excluded the substantive constitutional views of the opponents and thus Congress failed to have before it the overwhelming view of unconstitutionality. The reports are similarly slanted. The legislative process is equally faulty whether there are virtually no hearings, as was the fact for the Internet content laws discussed in chapter 2, or there are slanted hearings. The fact that subsequent administrations, even those philosophically in tune with the thinking behind Title II, have failed to embrace its provisions and have affirmatively resisted such an embrace demonstrates the defects of the result. Nevertheless, the law remains on the books.

Congress cannot be charged with irresponsibility or recklessness regarding the constitutionality of RFRA. The constitutional advice it received included respected scholars on both sides of the issue, and both sides were heard. However, both the language of the RFRA itself and the debate leading to it challenged the constitutional prerogatives and supremacy of the Supreme Court. The same was true of the debate leading to the enactment of Title II. Such an approach is constitutionally harmful.

7

Advisory Opinions and Other Proposed Remedies

One of the reasons often given by legislators to justify their reluctance to deal substantively with the constitutionality of proposed legislation is that they cannot determine the validity of constitutional claims with any degree of certainty. As Senator Henry Jackson of Washington put it, "it is an inescapable fact that fifty per cent of the lawyers are wrong in every law suit."[1] Statements such as "even lawyers and judges disagree" and "the Supreme Court may change its mind and not follow or distinguish earlier precedent" are often made to explain and justify the passage of what appears to be unconstitutional legislation. The argument goes: if those who ostensibly "know" the law and the Constitution cannot agree with certainty whether a bill is constitutional, how can a legislator, who often has no formal legal training, know what is constitutionally permissible? In response to these pleas, and ostensibly to provide constitutional certainty for the legislators, a number of states provide procedures that enable the legislatures to ask the highest state courts their opinions of the constitutionality of proposed bills.

A number of other "solutions" involving use of both the federal and state judiciary have also been made available. These approaches focus on the fact that when a law of doubtful constitutionality is passed a substantial amount of time usually passes before a lawsuit raising the constitutional issue is brought and decided by the courts. (Indeed, sometimes it is never brought.) The lapse of time between the passage of a law and the determination of its constitutionality by the courts undermines one of the purposes of law: to permit persons, business organizations, and other entities to be certain about the legality and effect of their behavior. During the period in which a statute's constitutionality has not yet been finally determined, expectations in relation to the law are not reliable. Citizens are uncertain whether to act in reliance on the statute. Financial investments, personnel decisions, business practice decisions, and sales practices are just some of the many kinds of behavior affected by laws. As a matter of public policy, it is undesirable to have a statute both effective because enacted and in limbo because its constitutionality has been challenged or is likely to be the subject of litigation. It is also undesirable to have on the books a law of questionable constitutional validity, which remains untested because of the cost of litigation or the unavailability of an appropriate person or entity to bring the legal action.

Attempts to mitigate the problem of lack of expectability using the courts include:

1. advisory opinions;
2. declaratory judgment actions;
3. accelerated judicial review and appeals to the Supreme Court provided as part of a constitutionally doubtful statute;
4. the bringing of test cases.

As the following discussion will demonstrate, neither advisory opinions nor postpassage judicial procedures solve the range of problems created by legislative abdication of constitutional responsibility; in fact, they create problems of their own.

Advisory Opinions

On a first cursory glance, it would seem that the obvious solution to the dilemma of the legislator struggling with doubts about a bill's constitutionality would be to have an advisory opinion by the highest court in response to an inquiry by the legislature. The legislature could ask, "Is this bill constitutional?" The court would respond yea or nay, as an advisor; thus, the name "advisory opinion." If the response were in the affirmative, the legislative branch could then address the policy issue of whether the bill was advisable or necessary without getting tangled up in questions of constitutionality, which often raise issues peripheral to the policy issues raised by the substance of the bill itself. If the response of the court were in the negative, the legislature could either shelve the bill or attempt to rewrite it to avoid the constitutional deficiencies raised by the court. In either case, the legislature would not be passing unconstitutional laws leading to costly and time-consuming litigation, as well as uncertainty during the period of litigation.

A review of the history and present status of advisory opinions at both the federal and state levels reveals that this supposed solution is not a panacea. The North Dakota Supreme Court quoted one of the participants in that state's constitutional convention, who said, "[T]here is not a state in the Union where that provision [for advisory opinions] prevails but not only the supreme court but every other person who has an intimate knowledge of the workings of that provision would wish it were not there."[2]

Those who support advisory opinions as a method of limiting the passage of unconstitutional law assume that unconstitutional laws are passed because of legislative ignorance regarding their constitutional status. While at times there may be genuine confusion or doubt, many of the examples I have discussed in previous chapters amply demonstrate that often, even when unconstitutionality is apparent or recognized, political considerations dictate the result and the proposal is enacted. In such a case, an advisory opinion would either not have been requested or would have been disregarded, as was other legal advice.

At present, advisory opinions are not available from the federal courts. Provisions explicitly granting the Supreme Court the power to advise were considered by the constitutional convention, but were not adopted.[3] Instead, Article III of the United States Constitution speaks only of "cases" and "controversies," which the Supreme Court has interpreted to mean issues presented in an adversary context. During the first few years after the adoption of the Constitution, the justices of the Supreme Court gave advice. For example, in response to a request from President George Washington, the justices advised that the statutory requirement that justices ride the circuit—that is, sit individually as a trial judge throughout the district to which they were assigned—was constitutionally questionable.[4] However, early in the 1790s the Supreme Court justices refused to advise Congress and the Secretary of War about certain pension matters.[5] And in 1793, in response to a written request of Secretary of State Thomas Jefferson in which he had set forth twenty-nine specific questions arising from the war between England and France, Chief Justice John Jay refused to advise President Washington and Secretary Jefferson on the interpretation of treaties with England and France.[6] The refusal was conveyed in a letter to Washington, stating, in a most polite way, that giving such advice would violate the constitutionally mandated separation of powers.

> We have considered the previous question stated in a letter written by your direction to us by the Secretary of State on the 18th of last month regarding the lines of separation drawn by the Constitution between the three departments of government. These being in certain respects checks upon each other, and our being Judges of a Court in the last resort, are considerations which afford strong arguments against the propriety of our extra-judicially deciding the questions alluded to, especially as the power given by the Constitution to the President, of calling on the heads of departments for opinions, seems to have been *purposely* as well as expressly limited to the *Executive* departments. We exceedingly regret every event that may cause embarrassment to your Administration, but we derive consolation from the reflection that your judgment will discern what is right, and that your usual prudence, decision and firmness will surmount every obstacle to the preservation of the rights, peace and dignity of the United States.[7]

Jay's position in this letter has remained the law to this time.

One notable and not fully explainable exception is worthy of mention. In 1822 President Monroe vetoed a bill that would have extended the federal power over turnpikes within the boundaries of a state, on the ground that it exceeded the power of the federal government. Before vetoing the bill, Monroe prepared in written form his constitutional rationale for the veto and sent a copy to each of the justices of the Supreme Court. Chief Justice Marshall replied, expressing agreement, Justice Story acknowledged receipt, and thereafter, Justice Johnson solicited and compiled the view of the justices and forwarded them to Monroe.[8]

From time to time since 1793, particularly during periods when the Supreme Court has disagreed with the Congress on issues, constitutional amendments have been proposed to permit or require advisory opinions by the Supreme Court. For example, as a result of the disputes over the constitutionality of various New Deal statutes in the 1930s, Congress attempted to pass legislation that would have required the Supreme Court to give advisory opinions. One proposal would have given the President or either house of Congress the power to request an opinion on constitutionality from the Court;[9] another would have given such power to the president and one-third of each of the houses of Congress;[10] and a third, far more radical, would have required the president to present every Act of Congress to the Supreme Court for constitutional review during a sixty-day period.[11] (The latter reminds one of the Council of Revision, established in the 1777 New York State Constitution.)[12] The efforts were unsuccessful, and neither these nor the others proposed at that time passed. Ultimately, as discussed later in this chapter, the concerns were mitigated to some extent by the expansion of the right of a litigant to seek a declaratory judgment and by statutory provisions providing for accelerated Supreme Court review of specified statutes.

On the other hand, at one time or another twenty-two state supreme courts had authority to provide advisory opinions under some circumstances.[13] Interestingly, almost half of these have discontinued the practice. Twelve continue to issue advisory opinions, although in one state the power is limited to capital punishment cases. In each of the states in which judicial advisory opinions are permissible, individualized procedures have been developed.

Given the desire of legislators, governors and the president for judicial guidance as part of the course of the legislation, why has the practice of using advisory opinions not expanded? Why, instead, has there been retreat from the procedure and uneasiness about using it?

There are some statutes that could have benefited from the availability of an advisory opinion. One such is the Legislative Line Item Veto Act signed by President Clinton on April 9, 1996,[14] which raised purely legal issues relating to the meaning of constitutional provisions. However, the potential usefulness of a hypothetical advisory opinion in determining the constitutionality of the Line Item Veto Act is the exception rather than the rule. The line item veto lawsuit is one of those few cases challenging the constitutionality of a statute that is not fact-sensitive. Usually, a constitutional challenge to a statute requires examination of the statute as it is applied to a variety of factual situations. With the Line Item Veto Act, however, one can almost lay the statute against section 7 of Article I, and then argue the meaning and intent of the constitutional provision as applied to the Act. Assuming that the procedure provided for briefing, arguments, and adequate time for consideration, an advisory opinion would have been apt.

History has demonstrated, however, that the benefits of the advisory opinion practice are generally outweighed by its practical problems. First and foremost, a request for an advisory opinion comes from one party (the governor, attorney general, or legislature). It does not set out contrary arguments or the variety of factual contexts in which the law could be applied. The court must explore the factual and legal ramifications on its own. In the context of our adversarial judicial system, substantive law and judicial procedure have developed in which two or more opposing parties refine the factual and legal disputes and present them to one or more judges for resolution. Even with the weaknesses of an adversarial system, such as missed issues or mismatched adversaries, a system of this kind raises issues far more effectively than a proceeding that is nonadversarial. One learns early in the practice of law that one cannot judge the merits of a matter merely from hearing information from a single source. Similarly, one cannot judge the merits of a matter merely from reading the brief of any one side. Only when opposing arguments have been presented can the relative merits of the parties be considered accurately.

Some of the courts that issue advisory opinions have attempted to create a more adversarial context by, in effect, hearing from all those who wish to be heard on the issue. This presumes, of course, that the court will have briefs and/or argument, which is not often the case, since to achieve the benefit of a speedy resolution the process often dispenses with both briefs and argument. The result is that most advisory opinions are triggered by a question, which is followed by a judicial response delivered, as it were, "*in vacuo.*"

While such a procedure does provide a response to the specific question posed, it is not likely to provide the most considered opinion to resolve the question posed in the first instance. Not only is there no adversarial consideration of the issues, but the question is usually considered divorced from any factual context. As Felix Frankfurter said while he was still a professor at Harvard Law School, before he was appointed to the Supreme Court:

> Since Reconstruction days, the acutest controversies which have come before our Supreme Court, and increasingly will come, ... concern, in effect, a delimitation between the powers of the Nation and those of the States and the eternal conflict between the freedom of the individual and his control by society. The stuff of these contests are facts, and judgment upon facts. Every tendency to deal with them abstractedly, to formulate them in terms of sterile legal questions, is bound to result in sterile conclusions unrelated to actualities. The reports are strewn with wrecks of legislation considered *in vacuo* and torn out of the context of life which evoked the legislation and alone made it intelligible.[15]

While the "context of life" when Frankfurter wrote these sentiments related to social legislation that was facing the scrutiny of a conservative U.S. Supreme Court, the recent attempt to legislate criminally enforced decency standards for the Internet under the rubric of the Communications Decency Act (CDA), subsequently struck down by the U.S. Supreme Court, demonstrates the validity of Frankfurter's point in the framework of a contemporary context of life.

The expressed purpose of the CDA was to protect children from both intended and inadvertent exposure to indecent materials on the Internet. The statute made it a crime to transmit "indecent" materials to a minor on the Internet. The CDA included provisions intended to provide for safe harbors that ostensibly would permit adults to receive all constitutionally protected speech, even if indecent. The CDA's constitutionality was challenged by various groups, including the ACLU and the American Library Association. For the hearing, the challengers had the courtroom wired for the Internet. Days of testimony were devoted to expert testimony demonstrating how the Internet actually worked, and how, based on that factual showing, the restrictions of the CDA would impede free speech. Based in great part on this very specific factual record, the trial court found the CDA unconstitutional, a decision that was affirmed by a unanimous Supreme Court.

It would have been quite different had the Supreme Court reviewed the CDA in an advisory capacity prior to its passage. The Court would not have had the benefit of the extensive factual record, but rather would have had to hypothesize the impact of the statute on speech, based on each individual justice's knowledge of the working of the Internet.

It is difficult to anticipate precisely what results will flow from a given piece of legislation. Often results are unanticipated by either the proponents or opponents of the legislation. Sometimes the results are beneficial; sometimes they are detrimental. In a case litigated between adversaries, the judges benefit from the knowledge, logic, and thinking of a number of persons, who themselves have been aided by others who have practical experience in the affected businesses or other areas. When an advisory opinion is given without the benefit of information, knowledge, and experience from those outside the judicial system, the potential for missing or misunderstanding the impact of the opinion and its constitutional implications is great.

It is not surprising, therefore, that when an issue previously "ruled" upon in an advisory opinion subsequently comes before the very same court in an actual adversary litigation, frequently the court issues an opinion that is at least to some extent inconsistent with its prior advice. The real facts and real parties represented by contesting advocates either raise issues that had not been previously considered when the advisory opinion was given or give the contemplated issues a different perspective. A fuller factual record can not only inform a court about constitutional infirmities that it had not contemplated. Early in this century the Massachusetts Supreme Judicial Court issued a number of advisory opinions raising constitutional issues; later, when faced with similar enacted legislation, the statutes were found to be constitutional.[16] In fact, Erwin Griswold, the former dean of Harvard Law School, when discussing the views of Felix Frankfurter and Justice Louis Brandeis noted:

> [T]he opposition of Justice Brandeis [to passing a federal declaratory judgment act]was largely based on his experience with the "Advisory Opinion" practice in Massachusetts, under which the Supreme Judicial Court of Massachusetts gives opinions on the constitutional validity of a statute before it is enacted into law. Because of Advisory Opinions, many constructive changes in the law of Massachusetts had been stopped in their tracks, without any opportunity for practical experience.
>
> Under the Advisory Opinion system, the constitutionality of a proposed statute is considered in vacuo. There is no actual case. There are no facts. There is no individual who has been hurt, or is being protected. There is a tendency for the court (and counsel in their argument) to hunt out the worst possible factual assumption, and to conclude that the statute, as drawn, would be invoked in such a case, leading to the result that the statute would be declared unconstitutional.
>
> Justice Brandeis and Professor Frankfurter felt that such a question should be considered by a court only in a concrete case, based on actual facts. Then, it might

be possible, in a trial, to present the factual background, to show what the statute would do to this particular plaintiff, and to present facts and arguments which would support the constitutionality of the statute as applied to those facts.[17]

Without a specific factual context and adversarial presentations, the philosophies of the members of the advising court may become paramount factors in the determination. Whether a proposal is constitutional or not depends on one's view of the bill in question. A civil libertarian viewing a bill as impinging on rights of free speech, a business leader concerned about restrictions on his freedom of contract, a union leader or a children's rights advocate seeking to advance a program of protections—each would have his or her particular views of a proposal affecting his or her own interests. Even that particular view might be modified or nuanced if the proposal were placed in a factual context. Similarly, the opinion of a court rendering an advisory opinion may unduly reflect the judge's philosophy. Further, if the advice of a supreme court is not a reliable predictor of the subsequent rulings of the very same court on the very same constitutional issue, the basis for seeking the advice in the first instance is substantially undermined.

Advisory opinions are usually described as being extrajudicial or nonjudicial, and therefore nonbinding. The advisory opinion is considered to be advice and counsel, similar to that which any lawyer gives to a client or an attorney general gives to a president or governor. The difference, of course, is that "advice" from a supreme court bears the apparent imprimatur of the supreme court, even though, in many of the states that provide for advisory opinions, the request is addressed to the justices in their individual capacities and the responses are presumed to be from them in such capacity. Nevertheless, the actuality of using designations such as "majority" and "dissent," and the fact that the advisory opinions are generally published along with the opinions of the court in litigated cases, leads one to treat the distinction between the court's opinions and the individual justices' opinions as a formal one. The perception of all parties, both governmental and public, is that it is the court that is giving the advice.

Whatever their actual value to decision making in future cases, advisory opinions are treated as if they were precedent, cited by courts and followed by them, absent any "new" facts or changes of constitutional doctrine. If advisory opinions were to be treated "merely" as advice, without binding precedential value, it would of course limit one of the major benefits claimed for the advisory opinion—that it settles the issue of constitutionality in a time- and cost-efficient manner prior to passage of the bill, so that thereafter persons can act or refrain from acting in reliance on the statute without fearing that it will subsequently be found unconstitutional. If the judicial advice cannot be relied on as the precursor of the later decision in postpassage litigation, this supposed benefit would be ephemeral. Why should a legislator rely, in deciding whether to vote for or against a given piece of legislation, upon "advice" from a group of lawyers simply because the lawyers happen to be justices of a supreme court? Unless the advice carries with it the benefit of predictability, the legislator could just as well seek the advice of a group of law deans or other constitutional scholars.

Another problem with the advisory opinion procedure arises from the need for a speedy response, which often prevents a thoughtful, considered analysis of the issue. (This is the flip side of the asserted advantage of speedy resolution of the outstanding issue.) A 1949 study found an average of thirty days from request for an advisory opinion to response by the state supreme court justices.[18] This speedy result is not surprising, because the requests are often time-sensitive. For example, of the nine advisory opinions requested of the North Carolina Supreme Court between 1947 and 1991, six related to the timing or content of forthcoming special or general elections.[19] Obviously, if the advice is not given sufficiently ahead of the election date to permit the ballot to be prepared or revised, the benefit of the advice is lost. Similarly, when a request is made of a court regarding a bill being considered by a legislature for passage or by a governor for signature, a time clock is generally running, either because the legislative session is drawing to a close, because an election is scheduled, or because practical political pressures are present.

This time pressure on the judges is harmful. It deprives them of the opportunity to consider thoughtfully the constitutional issues presented and whether there are other issues and concerns that are not immediately visible. By definition, constitutional issues relate to the society's core values and are worthy of considered thought. Constitutions, by their nature, are documents that use broad language needing interpretation. Many, including the United States Constitution, were drafted by framers who could not have anticipated contemporary issues, which often arise from scientific and technological developments. The answers to many constitutional questions are not simple and apparent.

The time pressure, as a practical matter, also prevents the justices from soliciting briefs and/or argument from interested parties, or imposes a briefing schedule that does not afford the lawyers the time they require to present the issues in depth. For both these reasons, time pressure may reduce the quality and the value of the advice given by the court and may make it more likely that subsequently, in a fully briefed, argued, and considered case, the court may reach a different result. This devalues not only the specific advisory opinion that is handed down but advisory opinions in general. Legislatures are less likely to seek or rely on such opinions, and it is more likely that any advisory opinion will be more susceptible to successful future challenge.

Significantly, there are policy reasons against broadening the use of the advisory opinion procedure. For one, the separation-of-powers doctrine embodied in state and federal constitutions represents not only a constitutional doctrine but also a policy decision—for some, growing out of the colonial experience—of the importance of checks and balances within the governmental structure. As was set forth in the Virginia Constitution of 1776: "The legislative, executive and judiciary departments shall be separate and distinct, so that neither exercise the powers properly belonging to the other: nor shall any person exercise the powers of more than one of them at the same time."[20] Separation of powers was, in fact, the basis of Chief Justice John Jay's refusal in 1793 to render an advisory opinion about treaty obligations to Washington and Jefferson.

Judges and the courts are ill equipped to participate in the legislative process. History has shown that some Supreme Court justices have continued to advise the executive, in a nonpublic manner, after their elevation to the Supreme Court bench.[21] Whatever the propriety of such actions may be, the inclusion of a supreme court as an institution or of the justices in their individual capacities into the legislative process is inconsistent with the separation of powers. From seeking the constitutional blessing of a court on proposed legislation, the legislature can easily move to seek judicial advice about an alternate formulation if the original proposal has constitutional defects. The role of a legislature is to determine and then implement policy. It negotiates with and attempts to reflect the varying concerns of the various groups in society, with the goal of adopting that which the legislature believes best meets the needs of the polity as a whole. This is not the goal and means of the judiciary, which has the duty of deciding adversary cases within the construct of a legal system, applying the Constitution and the laws which have been enacted.

The legislature and the executive each have an obligation to assess the constitutionality of legislation conscientiously and independently. Senator Robert Kennedy cogently argued that reliance on advisory opinions encourages avoidance of those obligations.[22] As Justice Frankfurter said, "Perhaps the most costly price of advisory opinions is the weakening of legislative and popular responsibility."[23] Whatever the validity of the view of those, like Robert Bork, who see democracy endangered because the "judicial usurpation of politics"[24] —an argument I find to be without merit—the intrusion of the judiciary into the process of legislation through advisory opinions shifts to judges and courts that which was clearly and properly given to the legislative branch. Courts are and should remain adjudicatory, rather than advisory, bodies.

Further, imposing advisory functions on the courts diminishes the independence of the judiciary which is so important for the protection of constitutional rights. When advisory opinions are permitted, it is the legislature or the executive that determines whether a request is to be made, the timing of the request, and the substance of the request itself. While there have been a number of instances of state supreme courts declining to grant a particular advisory opinion, even though they may acknowledge their general obligation to issue such opinions, the power to choose the subject matter and timing of the request remains the prerogative of the two other branches. Many of the advisory opinions relate to highly politicized issues. Referring such issues to a supreme court, the members of which often are elected for a stated term of office, has the effect of passing the hot potato to the judiciary. It is thus not surprising that even those courts which retain advisory powers have continued to restrict and delimit their use.

In sum, the apparent benefits of advisory opinions—both in helping legislators meet their constitutional obligations and, more generally, in providing the political system with a procedure for the speedy and efficient resolution of constitutional questions—are not that clear-cut and are outweighed by the demerits of that procedure.

Before moving on, we should look at three other avenues for testing constitutional infirmities—cases seeking a declaratory judgment, accelerated appeal procedures for statutes which the legislature recognizes to be constitutionally suspect, and "test cases." All three differ from advisory opinions in that they are actually litigated lawsuits, with one or more plaintiffs bringing the action and one or more defendants resisting it. They are also different in that they do not give legislators guidance to the passage of a possibly unconstitutional law; rather they attempt to mitigate the post-passage impact of such a law by expediting the process of judicial decision making, generally by the accelerating the commencement of the litigation. Like advisory opinions, their purpose is to seek a court determination regarding the constitutionality of legislation without waiting for the happenstance of a case whose facts raise the issue.

Declaratory Judgments

A suit for a declaratory judgment is unusual in that it seeks to resolve a controversy with a statement by a court about a legal issue, such as whether a statute is constitutional or a contract remains in force. Normally, a party bringing a lawsuit seeks some form of palpable relief, such as an order to pay money or an order to the defendant to do or not to do something (referred to as an injunction). In an action for a declaratory judgment, two parties to a contract who disagree whether the contact remains in force can seek a declaration to resolve the issue before either party has to take an action that might constitute a breach of the contract. In the context of a statute, the suit can be brought by a party regulated or restricted by a civil or criminal statute who believes the statute to be unconstitutional. Although no action has been brought to enforce the statute or to punish any potentially offending party, a declaratory judgment action is brought to raise the question of the constitutionality of the statute. If the enforcer of or regulator under the statute is an agency of government, the case is brought against the appropriate agency.

Declaratory judgments to challenge constitutionality may not be available if the statute gives a right of action to a class of private persons. Thus the Dworkin/MacKinnon anti-pornography ordinance discussed in chapter 3, in addition to granting rights and powers to an agency of the city of Indianapolis, granted *any woman* the right to sue persons deemed to violate the civil rights of women generally by the distribution of material found to depict the sexual subordination of women. If that had been all that the ordinance included, it would have been difficult for plaintiffs to identify an appropriate defendant for a declaratory judgment action. *All* women of Indianapolis could not have been sued; nor could one random person as representative of the class of women generally be sued. In the Indianapolis case the problem was avoided, since the most of the enforcement obligations fell upon the city—an obviously appropriate defendant in a suit. Had the granting of rights to women generally been a freestanding ordinance, one might have had to wait until a suit had been brought under the ordinance.

Although legal historians trace the concept of declaratory relief back to Roman law, the American versions find their parentage in English developments in the late nineteenth century.[25] The first comprehensive declaratory judgment statute in the United States was passed by New Jersey in 1915.[26] In 1922, the National Conference of Commissioners on Uniform State Laws proposed a Uniform Declaratory Judgments Act, which has been substantially adopted by most states.[27] Other states have developed their own forms of statutes permitting declaratory relief. After years of discussion, the federal Declaratory Judgment Act was passed in 1934.[28]

The primary intent of the Uniform Act and the state laws that followed it was not to provide a forum for testing statutory constitutionality. Rather, the acts had a commercial and personal focus. The Uniform Act refers specifically only to construing contracts, deeds, and wills, and to providing executors, trustees, and the like with a venue to define their obligations. Constitutional issues come within a catchall provision stating that the enumeration of cases is not exclusive. The federal act is more general in scope and includes no such specification.

The federal Civil Rights Act of 1871, enacted during the Reconstruction Era, is another federal statute which, in conjunction with the declaratory judgment act, can be used to test the constitutionality of a state statute. As the U.S. Supreme Court stated, one of the purposes of the Act was, in fact, to provide a remedy in the federal courts against unconstitutional state laws.[29] Codified as § 1983 of Title 42 of the federal laws, this statute has provided the legal foundation for many attacks on unconstitutional state laws.

While § 1988 of the 1871 Act provides monetary recompense for the expenses of a successful challenge under § 1983, mitigating cost as a deterrent to the lawsuit, a suit to strike an unconstitutional statute, brought under the Declaratory Judgment Act and/or § 1983, does not eliminate or even substantially shorten the postpassage life of an unconstitutional statute. A lawsuit brought just prior to the effective date of the infirm statute, if carried to the Supreme Court, will, under the most favorable scenario, last for two or three years. Although in some instances the trial court will enjoin the effectiveness of the statute pending determination of its constitutionality, the uncertainty remains. While the availability of declaratory judgment procedures is thus not, even under the best of circumstances, a cure for the constitutional recklessness of legislators, it can be a relatively prompt method to limit the harm.

Accelerated Appeals

Recently, when faced with political or social pressure to pass a statute of doubtful constitutionality, federal legislators have on occasion inserted into such a law a provision for an accelerated hearing and appeal to the Supreme Court. Such a provision, it is suggested, mitigates the potential harm of passing an unconstitutional law. It is almost as if, prevented by the Constitution from being able to obtain an advisory opinion, Congress attempts at least to provide a court decision shortly after passage. From a more cynical point of view, it is another way of shifting the unpleasant task of saying no to the judiciary while at the same time appearing cautious and sensitive to constitutional concerns. There does not seem to be any readily visible substantive basis for distinguishing those constitutional doubtful statutes to which Congress appends an accelerated appeal provision and those that do not include such a provision. The decision appears to be purely political. When an accelerated remedy provision is considered politically advisable to procure the necessary votes, avoid or override a presidential veto, or simply appear "reasonable" to the opposition, it is included; otherwise, it is not included.

In the recent Line Item Veto Act, section 3, entitled "Judicial Review," begins with a subsection entitled "Expedited Review":

> Any Member of Congress or any individual adversely affected by [the Line Item Veto Act] . . . may bring an action, in the United States District Court for the District of Columbia, for declaratory judgment and injunctive relief on the ground that any provision of [the Act] . . . violates the Constitution.[30]

The next subsection provides that any appeal from the decision of the District Court shall be directly to the Supreme Court, bypassing the intermediate Court of Appeals.[31] Finally, a subsection headed "Expedited Consideration" reads:

> It shall be the duty of the District Court for the District of Columbia and the Supreme Court of the United States to advance on the docket and to expedite to the greatest possible extent the disposition of any matter brought under . . . [this section].[32]

Congress, having passed a statute that it recognized to be of doubtful constitutionality, instructed the federal courts, including the Supreme Court, that it is the "duty" of the courts to expedite constitutional review in order to minimize the harm that Congress has caused.

In the Communications Decency Act, also passed by the 104th Congress, there is a provision entitled "Expedited Review" which reads:

(a) THREE-JUDGE DISTRICT COURT HEARING—Notwithstanding any other provision of law, any civil action challenging the constitutionality, on its face, of ... [the CDA], or any provision thereof, shall be heard by a district court of 3 judges. ...

(b) APPELLATE REVIEW—Notwithstanding any other provision of law, an interlocutory or final judgment, decree, or order of the court of 3 judges in an action under subsection (a) holding ... [the CDA], or ... any provision thereof, unconstitutional shall be reviewable as a matter of right by direct appeal to the Supreme Court.[33]

Unfortunately, the mechanism turns out to be neither speedy nor efficient, even when, as in the case of these two statutes, there are groups ready, willing, and able to mount the challenge. The Line Item Veto Act was signed by President Clinton on April 9, 1996. The initial challenge, by six members of Congress, although successful at the trial court level,[34] was dismissed by the Supreme Court on June 27, 1997.[35] The Act's constitutionality—or rather its unconstitutionality—was announced by the Supreme Court on April 27, 1998, in an appeal from a different challenge, over two years after the Act had been signed. In the interim President Clinton had exercised the line item veto eight-two times to eliminate $1.9 billion of spending.

The Communications Decency Act (CDA) was signed by President Clinton in February 1996. Three cases were brought challenging the CDA, two in Philadelphia (one by the ACLU and one by a group of media entities spearheaded by the American Library Association) and one in New York by an internet publisher. The Philadelphia cases were consolidated and heard together. The special three-judge trial court provided for in the expedited review provision that heard the Philadelphia cases issued its decision holding the statute unconstitutional on July 11, 1996, and the Supreme Court upheld that ruling on July 2,1997. The cases had been pressed forward to the utmost, despite their complexity. Nevertheless, the law was on the books for more than sixteen months.[36]

Thus, while an accelerated appeal provision may give the appearance of allaying constitutional concerns, it is only speedy in that a full-fledged litigation would take even longer. It is also costly. Finally, as noted earlier, the pressure on the court system for a speedy result may itself have deleterious effects.

Test Cases

Test cases are much like suits for a declaratory judgment, except that they involve a specific factual situation, albeit sometimes created for the purpose of the suit. A well-known example was the Scopes "monkey" trial, which brought Clarence Darrow to Dayton, Tennessee, to litigate the constitutionality of the Tennessee statute prohibiting the teaching of evolution ("that denies the story of the Divine Creation of man as taught in the Bible and . . . teach[es] instead that man has descended from a lower order of animals") in the public schools. Darrow's adversary was William Jennings Bryan. John T. Scopes was a local public school teacher who had agreed to teach evolution and be arrested to test the constitutionality of the statute.[37]

Even when a willing sacrificial lamb is available to be defendant, test cases suffer the same defects described earlier with respect to declaratory judgments. They occur after the contested law has gone into effect and can be lengthy. In contrast to declaratory judgments, the effect of the contested law often cannot be stayed during the litigation. In addition, it is often difficult to find a person to become the subject of a test case, particularly when a prison sentence or significant monetary damages could be imposed on the defendant, or when the defendant is likely to face public opprobrium. Finally, when a test case has been prepared, governmental officials may choose not to bring a charge or action under the statute that is intended to be challenged. The prospective test case defendant and the surrounding circumstances are often selected to present a scenario that demonstrates the infirmities and harshness of the challenged statute, thereby showing it in its least favorable light. Recognizing this, government officials may prefer to wait until a case that has circumstances demonstrating the good reasons for the passage of the law can be brought.

While the "remedies" for the irresponsible passage of unconstitutional legislation discussed in this chapter may mitigate some of the unfortunate ramifications of such action, they do not overcome the harm of such irresponsible action.

8

Conclusion

Unconstitutional laws are irresponsibly passed by legislatures in violation of the legislators' constitutional oath for a variety of reasons: ignorance of the subject matter under consideration because full and fair hearings, or any hearings at all, have not been conducted; political benefits that cause the legislators to ignore the issue of constitutionality; and legislators' beliefs that Supreme Court precedents are wrongly decided and therefore not worthy of compliance, that constitutionality is an issue not for them but for judicial resolution, or that the obligation of a legislator is to vote the desires of constituents, regardless of the constitutional standing of the constituent, desired legislation.[1] In the examples discussed in this book, each of these reasons has been involved, directly or indirectly.

The irresponsible passage of unconstitutional legislation is harmful to our system of government. In many challenges to such statutes, the defenders of the law present the Constitution as an impediment to, rather than the foundation of, good government. When the attack is upon the courts, particularly the Supreme Court, the challenge inherently constitutes an attack on the Constitution and the doctrine of separation of powers. The unwillingness of legislators, both state and federal, to consider seriously the constitutionality of legislation when it is not politically expedient to do so constitutes an abdication of their constitutional responsibilities in the most fundamental sense: it undermines, for political and selfish motives, the system they are sworn to serve.

The frequent lack or inadequacy of hearings when laws of doubtful constitutionality are enacted is worthy of particular comment. In models of governance, the legislative branch is considered to have a superior institutional capacity to collect evidence. Legislators cannot possibly be experts in all matters that may be the subject of legislation. They must rely on the information and advice of those who are or claim to be knowledgeable, and with expert help sort valid considerations from those that are not valid. Through committee staffs and legislative hearings, legislatures are well equipped to carry on effective fact-finding.[2] As the United States Supreme Court has said, the legislature "is far better equipped than the judiciary to amass and evaluate the vast amounts of data bearing on legislative questions."[3] Hearings and other fact-finding procedures serve at least five purposes in the legislative evaluation of proposed litigation.

1. They help in the consideration of whether a suggested policy and its substantive result are desirable.
2. They help in the appraisal of whether the proposed legislation will achieve the desired policy and its substantive result.
3. They help to discover unintended consequences.
4. They help in the analysis of whether the proposed legislation will, in concept or application, conflict with any constitutional restriction.
5. They help in the effort to provide an opportunity to the public and knowledgeable persons not otherwise consulted by the legislators to testify about issues or infor-

mation not raised by those who were consulted by the legislators.

Conducting hearings that are substantively partisan or failing to conduct hearings at all prevents consideration not only of constitutional issues but also of policy and substantive issues. Legislators cannot make reasoned decisions without knowledge of the underlying information, options, and consequences. This is quite obvious when contemporary scientific, medical, and technological issues are before the legislature. Help is needed, too, for problems that have long been with us, concerning issues such as education and crime prevention.

The fact that a legislature has both the capability and the responsibility to carry out effective and responsible fact-finding does not mean that it will happen. As we saw in chapter 2, Congress, when faced with the novelty and complexity of the Internet, designed a scheme for content regulation without the benefit of any hearings whatsoever. This moved the locus of fact-finding to the courts. After the Communications Decency Act had been held unconstitutional by every judge who considered the issue, in 1998 Congress passed the Child Online Protection Act (COPA).[4] Again Congress acted without hearings and without any information-based fact-finding, although the statute includes conclusory legislative "findings of fact" responsive to some of the deficiencies found by courts when they struck down the CDA. Instead of collecting information before passage, as part of COPA Congress established a Commission on Online Child Protection, primarily composed of industry members chosen by the Speaker of the House and the Majority Leader of the Senate. The responsibility given to the commission is to consider methods to help reduce minors' access to harmful material on the Internet and to report to Congress one year later.[5] The report of the commission, originally due in 1999, but now substantially delayed both by pending litigation and lack of appointments to the commission, will address the factual issues that underlie COPA, the act passed more than a year earlier. In effect, Congress enacted the law first and intended to have the fact-finding done by a nonlegislative body during the following year: the cart is really before the horse.

One might ask why we should be concerned about the passage of unconstitutional legislation if ultimately errors are corrected by the courts. Simply, judicial review cannot provide the way to resolve many of these foundational issues. Some unconstitutional laws remain on the books and in fact are never challenged, either because the impact of such laws—their economic and/or philosophical impact—is not great enough to justify the cost of a court challenge, or because there does not happen to be anyone willing to lead such a challenge who has the required legal status or standing, or because those affected by the law do not have the legal knowledge to recognize its unconstitutionality and do not have access to those who do have such knowledge. The statute overriding the Supreme Court's *Miranda* decision might fall into this category.

Even if an unconstitutional law is ultimately successfully challenged and stricken down by the courts, it usually has been on the books for some period of time—usually years. During that period, unless a court has stayed its effectiveness, the law controls the conduct of businesses and individuals. If the statute criminalizes conduct, those regulated must desist from the activity pending invalidation of the law by the courts. (In the context of statutes violating the First Amendment, this effect is called the "chilling effect" of self-censorship.) If the statute is noncriminal, but regulatory, those subject to it will make business and personal decisions based on an unconstitutional edict; when the unconstitutional act is subsequently nullified, these personal and business decisions often cannot be reversed; opportunities, creative ventures, scientific development, personal fortunes are lost: what's done is done.

There is also the cost of a constitutional challenge, in time, in money, and in the stress imposed on the litigating challenger. Anyone who has been a party to such a litigation knows the time and psychological demands it imposes. On top of those demands are the direct financial requirements. The recent successful challenge to the Communications Decency Act—the federal law passed in 1996 to prohibit children's access to "indecent" material on the Internet—cost over $1,500,000 even though the CDA provided for an accelerated procedure for the challenge that was intended to limit both time and cost. Although the CDA challenge involved large corporations with significant resources, even the economically well off should not be needlessly required to fund expensive challenges to defend their constitutional rights. Nor should the costs be multiplied by the need to bring multiple lawsuits repeatedly challenging defective laws on the same subject.

Further, it should not be a surprise that many of the unconstitutional laws that are passed violate the rights of the politically weak or unpopular, those least likely to have either the resources or the organization to mount a constitutional challenge.

Of utmost significance is the festering harm to our system of government. The irresponsible passage of an unconstitutional law is an attack by one or more parts of the government—a government that was established to protect and foster the rights of its citizens—on those very rights and citizens. The passage of unconstitutional or ineffective legislation promotes unhealthy cynicism for the legislative process when it becomes clear that legislators have voted for legislation for the short-term political benefit with the knowledge that it will be invalidated by the courts. The irresponsible passage of unconstitutional statutes, often followed by attacks on the courts for thwarting the will of the people's representatives, as in the Missouri family-planning example discussed in chapter 5, is harmful to the judicial branch of government. The courts are attacked and demeaned as providing "runaway justice" and having overstepped their bounds when, in fact, in many cases the unconstitutional laws were passed with the knowledge and expectation that the courts would do precisely what they did. As we have seen, legislatures, when faced with difficult political and substantive issues, often find it easier to pass simplistic but popular laws rather than deal with the complex and often politically unattractive nuances of the issue. It is easier from a political point of view to argue as if the issues of the day are starkly one way or the other rather than nuanced.

Not only is the antijudicial rhetoric generally unjustified; it distracts the public from the fact that there is a substantive problem to be solved or a real concern to be alleviated. Such rhetoric, most recently from the political right, is both a ploy to distract the public from seeing the legislature's inability or unwillingness to deal with difficult problems and an attempt to seek minimization of constitutional strictures. Rather than blaming the courts for standing in the way of solutions to important public issues, legislators should be seeking creative solutions within constitutional bounds.

It is important to discourage the knowing or reckless passage of unconstitutional legislation while not stifling legitimate legislative experimentation and creativity. There are structural and institutional Band-Aids that are moderately helpful. For one, there are statutes, most notably under the federal Civil Rights Act[6] and the Equal Access to Justice Act,[7] that provide for plaintiffs challenging an unconstitutional statute to be reimbursed for all or part of their legal fees and costs if they are successful. These provisions are important and necessary since otherwise many constitutional challenges would not be brought. In my experience, however, the fear of having to pay plaintiffs' legal fees has not proven to be a significant deterrent, except for smaller municipalities for whom the potential reimbursement would be material. The costs are not chargeable to the legislators or to the legislature, but rather to the political entity—city, state, or nation. While there is a surface appeal to making legislators (or at least the legislative sponsors) fiscally responsible for costs of successful challenges to their unconstitutional legislation, it would be impractical and harmful to the legislative process. The potential liability is likely to be so material for a legislator as to cause him or her not to vote for a bill whenever those who oppose the bill threaten a court challenge. The other available pre-passage mechanism is the advisory opinion. As the discussion in chapter 7 demonstrates, that is a flawed approach.

What is necessary is that federal, state, and municipal legislators recognize and abide by their constitutional obligation to act reasonably to avoid sponsoring or voting for unconstitutional laws. In many cases the problem is not caused by uncertainty about the meaning and impact of the constitutional restrictions: time and again unconstitutionality is acknowledged, explicitly or implicitly. But even when the law is less clear, the amount and level of assistance available to those in Congress is extensive. Similarly, most state legislators have legislative counsel, staff, and other agencies available. If state and federal legislators were to make use of the full panoply of available support services, including public hearings, for a better and deeper knowledge of the issues raised, both substantive and constitutional, many of the problems discussed in this book, and the cynicism of the legislative process that results, would be alleviated. This would require resisting the temptation to follow the easy political route. There are problems, such as pornography, terrorism, drugs, and violent crime, for which there seems to be a political imperative to legislate strongly and simply, even though the legislation may be unconstitutional and/or ineffective. As elections approach, the political pressures for such actions increase.

Legislators must accept the fact that the will of their constituents is subject to the mandate of the Constitution; in their leadership roles, legislators must endeavor to make voters aware of this. For legislators and legislatures to regain and maintain their appropriate stature, and for the appropriate continuance of the separation of powers, the easy political way must be resisted.

Statistical Appendix

Analysis of a Survey of Legislators, Legislative Counsels, and Offices of the Attorneys General

This survey owes a considerable debt to Donald G. Morgan's *Congress and the Constitution,* which concluded with an analysis of a short survey Morgan had conducted of federal legislators.[1] Both this survey and Morgan's provide broad analyses of the ways in which the players in the legislative process understand their various roles and responsibilities; therefore, to a certain extent, they add another dimension to the conclusions that can be drawn from the various examples discussed in this book. Whereas Morgan solicited information only from U.S. Senators and members of Congress, the present survey was distributed to selected state legislators, state legislative counsels, and offices of the states' attorneys general, as well.

Five of the six questions Morgan asked were incorporated into the present survey. This was done because many of the Morgan's questions were well crafted, continued to be germane, and, as the source of a new data set, provided the longitudinal backdrop for some comparisons across time. It should also be noted, however, that the two surveys differ notably in the populations they investigated and the questions they pose. I shall address each of these differences in this order.

Comparisons between the survey data gathered here and by Morgan, although still useful, are limited by one important difference, those who were solicited and responded. While 203 of 538 federal legislators responded to Morgan, only 12 of the 438 members of Congress responded this time; no Senators responded, though a few letters were received from their staff.[2]

On the other hand, the rate of return from state legislators and officials—87 of approximately 200—was better than Morgan's percentage of return from federal legislators and, obviously, provides more broadly based information than did the responses Morgan received. As in Morgan's study, there was little self-selection bias. The responses received were nearly evenly split between counselors—legislative counsel, governors' counsel, and attorneys general—(52 percent) and legislators (48 percent). Of the state legislators, 42 percent were state senators and 58 percent were members of the lower houses. The breakdown in the set of counselors was 64 percent from the offices of attorneys general, 21 percent from governors' counsels, and 15 percent from state legislative counsels.[3] As to political affiliation, 52 percent of legislators identified themselves as Republicans and 48 percent identified themselves as Democrats, while only 38 percent of counselors identified themselves as Republicans and 62 percent identified themselves as Democrats. Taken as a total, the distribution was quite balanced, with 47 percent of respondents identified as Republicans and 53 percent identified as Democrats. They were also well distributed across geographic region, with all regions participating, and the tallies loosely[4] reflecting contemporary American demographics: 11 percent of our responses came from New England; 8 percent from Middle Atlantic states; 28 percent from the Midwest; 8 percent from border states; 19 percent from the South; and 24 percent from the Far West.[5]

Another important difference between the two surveys was their length. Morgan's study was limited to six questions and fit on one side of a page, while the present survey posed twenty questions to legislators and seventeen to counselors, fitting them on two sides of a page.[6] The present survey chose five of Morgan's six questions.[7] In this appendix I have analyzed the responses received to six of the most central questions.

Since a basic issue is how legislators and their counsels understood the distribution of the task of constitutional determination between the various branches, the survey inquired, as had Morgan's:

Generally speaking, should a legislature pass constitutional questions along to the courts rather than form its own considered judgment on them?

Legislative judgment	Legislator[8]	Counselor[8]	All[8]
Yes	15%	9%	11%
No	68%	65%	64%
No opinion	18%	27%	24%

The results are quite clear: an overwhelming number of legislators and counselors believe that it is within the scope of legislative responsibility to consider the constitutional aspects of proposed legislation. Morgan, referring to this as the "tripartite" theory of constitutional responsibility, noted its abiding adherence to Article VI of the United States Constitution.[9] When Morgan asked the question of federal legislators, nearly twice the rate—31 percent—responded yes. The percentage responding no to Morgan was not markedly different from this survey, since only a few responded "No Opinion."[10] The number of respondents who marked "No Opinion" has thus appreciably risen, perhaps indicating less certainty in these times or at the state and local level.[11]

The survey also adopted a rather sharp question from Morgan:

When constitutional questions are raised, are they likely to be bona fide issues or political maneuvers?

Constitutional questions	Legislator	Counselor	All
Bona fide issues	74%	41%	65%
Political maneuvers	0%	18%	17%
Both	18%	18%	
No opinion	9%	24%	19%

The disparity between the responses of legislators and counselors is most striking, with the former purporting to be far more certain of the bona fide nature of the issues raised. There are several possible explanations for this difference. The first, referred to perhaps uncharitably here as "cynical," is that legislators are unwilling to classify as constitutional bad faith a tactic that they may themselves use. Alternatively, a "naive" explanation would suggest that legislators, as those who closest to the business of drafting and proposing legislation, are best able, even when compared to those who most often provide them constitutional advice, to assess their own intentions when raising constitutional claims. Furthermore, a cynical explanation can also be applied to the claims of counselors: counselors have a stake in shaming legislators into dependence upon them.[12] Finally, I have often heard, particularly from members of Congress, the statement that constitutional issues have been raised as a political chip and thus should not be taken seriously. Whether the survey represents a different perspective at the state level is not clear, although, in Morgan's day, 30 percent of responding federal legislators indicated that appeals to the Constitution are likely to be politically motivated.[13] It should be noted that, although the option of "both" was not made available on the present survey or on Morgan's, a significant number—18 percent in the present survey and 16 percent in Morgan's—chose to hedge their responses by acting as if it had been included as a survey choice.

The next question, also taken from Morgan, sought to gauge the degree to which legislators, who heard the testimony of constitutional "experts," the opinions of civic leaders, and each other's views, are motivated by a good faith, open-minded appraisal of the best constitutional arguments put before them.

Do you think that debates or committee discussions on constitutional questions have significant influence on the voting on those questions? (This question only appeared on the legislative survey.)

Yes	76%
No	21%
No opinion	3%

While the results were overwhelming in their support for

the meaningfulness of constitutional debate and discussion, having fully one-fifth of responses indicate the contrary is remarkable, considering the commonsense understandings of the ways in which politics and the legislative process are to be conducted in a democracy.[14] In Morgan's day, however, legislators were even less receptive to such process: 67 percent believed that discussion and debate was meaningful, and 33 percent believed that they were not.[15]

The next logical step along this line of inquiry was also borrowed from Morgan. After the inquiry about the meaningfulness of testimony that informs legislators, the survey asked what sort of respect courts ought to afford to the determinations of the legislature. After all, if one adopts the "tripartite" perspective, every branch of government must be mindful of the constitutionality of its actions, and it would benefit the conceptual integrity of the system, taken as a functioning whole, for the findings of each to be granted some standing by the others.

When the courts are called on to decide a constitutional question, how much weight do you think they should attach to an earlier determination of the same question by the legislature?

Weight	Legislator	Counselor	All	Morgan
No weight at all	27%	29%	28%	16%
Limited weight	42%	45%	44%	40%
A great deal of weight	27%	26%	27%	40%
Controlling weight	3%	0%	1%	4%

While respondents believed that legislators ought to consider the constitutionality of legislation, less than a majority thought that the courts should give significant weight to the "determinations" rendered by legislatures. Interestingly, the

Morgan study found respondents suggesting a higher regard for the work of legislators, with 40 percent marking "a great deal" and only 16 percent marking "no weight at all," despite the more cynical views they expressed regarding the quality of legislative discourse. The difference may well be attributable to the greater self-esteem of federal, as opposed to state, legislators; whether justified or not, they may consider themselves as having a greater responsibility for the maintenance of constitutional standards than do state legislators.

How informed are legislators on constitutional matters?

Level of being informed	Legislator	Counselor	All
Well informed	15%	9%	12%
Well enough informed	50%	65%	58%
Poorly informed	35%	25%	30%

Perhaps the single most significant addition of the present survey was the following question, seeking to have respondents indicate the priority of the legislative role as either a representative of their consistents or as keepers of the constitutional faith.

Which of the following statements would you regard as true?

Legislators have a greater responsibility to their constituents . . .

Legislator	Counselor	All
61%	60%	61%

Legislators have a greater responsibility to Supreme Court decisions . . .

	Legislator	Counselor	Total
	35%	40%	38%
Other	3%	1%	4%

Both legislators and counselors chose, in significant proportion, to give priority to direct, popular rule over their duty to legislate in a constitutional manner as determined by court rulings.

Taken as a whole, the survey findings presented here can be combined into a model of legislative and judicial decision making that is both coherent and consistent with the prior discussion in this book. First, despite their constitutional oath, legislators are primarily informed by the will of their constituents and secondarily informed by the considerations of even the highest judicial body, the Supreme Court. Second, views of the legislature enacting laws need not be given special standing by the judiciary. If legislators believe the judges need not be bound by legislative views of constitutionality, it may be inferred that legislators believe they are similarly not bound by judges' constitutional decisions. Each branch is free to apply its own judgments, standards, and references.

Interestingly, the model of government in which legislators follow the people and the courts decide independent of legislative actions takes into account a somewhat cynical view of the role of the Constitution in legislative debate, while it also reinforces the notion that the legislature is the body closest to "the People" and, therefore, occupies a special role in government. As considered in the conclusion, however, this model of governmental process is deeply problematic. For one, the model is not faithful to the oath of office that all legislators must take. Secondly, if *Marbury v. Madison* establishes the Court as the final arbiter of constitutional meaning and legislatures unjustifiably refuse to follow that lead, we are left with instability at the core. Of course, one can expect some institutional drift in the ensuing two hundred years. Nevertheless, our governing understanding of the role of the Supreme Court as the ultimate constitutional arbiter does not allow for such unauthorized and self-aggrandizing reinterpretation on the part of legislators.[16] For legislators to minimize the rulings of the Supreme Court in their determination of the constitutionality of proposed legislation is a misconception of their constitutional obligation.

Notes

Introduction

1. Act of June 1, 1789, 1 Stat. 23.
2. The original oath was fourteen words long and simply paraphrased the constitutional requirement. The present oath, which is substantially longer, modifies and perhaps limits the obligation to support the Constitution by appending "against all enemies foreign and domestic" to the obligation to support. It also adds the obligation to "bear true faith and allegiance to the" Constitution. 5 U.S.C. § 3331.
3. For a twentieth-century comparison, the French Fifth Republic permits the executive and judicial branches to disagree as to the substantive meaning of the Constitution, with the result dependent on the body before which the dispute is heard. See Burt Neuborne, "Judicial Review and Separation of Powers in France and the United States," 57 *N.Y.U. L. Rev.* 363 (1982).
4. Donald G. Morgan, Congress and the Constitution: A Study of Responsibility *(Cambridge: Harvard University Press, 1966),* 10-11.
5. 104 Cong. Rec. S12468 (June 27, 1958).
6. Fort Lauderdale (Florida) *News,* January 17, 1984, 1, 10A.
7. The issue was whether Jehovah's Witnesses were excused from compliance with compulsory flag salute exercises in public schools because their religion viewed such action as saluting a graven image. In *Minersville School District v Gobitis,* 310 U.S. 586 (1940), a divided Supreme Court held that the Witnesses must comply. Three years later, in *West Virginia State Board of Educ. v Barnette,* 319 U.S. 624 (1943), the Court, by a vote of 6-3, reversed its prior decision.
8. *Miranda v Arizona,* 384 U.S. 436 (1966).
9. Controlling Crime Through More Effective Law Enforcement: Hearings Before the Subcomm. on Criminal Law and Procedure of the Senate Comm. on the Judiciary, 90th Cong., 1st Sess. (1967), 2138.
10. *United States v Dickerson,* 166 F.3d 667 (4th Cir. 1999).

11. Introduction to Symposium, "The End of Democracy? The Judicial Usurpation of Politics," *First Things* (November 1996), 18.
12. See, for example, the proposals cited in Max Baucus and Kenneth R. Kay, "The Court Stripping Bills: Their Impact on the Constitution, the Courts, and Congress," 27 *Vill. L. Rev.* 988, 992 n.18 (1982).
13. Robert H. Bork, "Our Judicial Oligarchy," in Symposium, "The End of Democracy" The Judicial Usurpation of Politics," *First Things*, November 1966, 23.
14. Linda Greenhouse of the *New York Times* has highlighted another aspect of the problem, the passage of statutes by Congress setting a policy but not setting forth the subordinate detail. Such statutes, in effect, delegate the delineation of the details of application to administrative agencies and the courts. Greenhouse, "Sure Justices Legislate. They Have To," *New York Times*, July 5, 1998.
15. Even when the legislature provides for an expedited constitutional appeals procedure, as Congress did in 1996 with the Communications Decency Act, and even when the expedited procedure is followed, a resolution will require more than a year.
16. *First Things*, November 1996, 18.
17. Glen Johnson, "Deciding Abortion, Suicide Issues Is Duty of Congress, Scalia Says," *Washington Post*, March 10, 1998, A7.
18. Louis Michael Seidman and Mark Tushnet, *Remnants of Belief: Contemporary Issues* (New York: Oxford University Press, 1996).
19. In April 1999, Governor Gray Davis of California tried to reach a middle ground by appealing a court decision holding unconstitutional a proposition denying health, education, and welfare benefits to illegal immigrants, while at the same time asking the appellate court's mediation panel to mediate the dispute. "I'm a governor, not a judge. I have taken an oath to enforce all of the laws of our state and nation, regardless of my personal views on those laws." Noah Isackson, "Court May Hear Immigration Dispute," *AP OnLine*, April 16, 1999.
20. See *Arizonans for Official English v Arizona*, 520 U.S. 43 (1997).

1 A Brief Historical Overview

1. *Northern Pipeline Constr. Co. v Marathon Pipe Line Co.*, 458 U.S. 50, 60 (1982).
2. See, e.g. Richard H. Cox, introduction to *Four Pillars of Constitutionalism* (Amherst, N.Y.: Prometheus, 1998), at 58-61.
3. Scholars differ on this issue of the Constitution carrying out the principles of the Declaration of Independence. Sotirious A. Barber, *The Constitution of Judicial Power* (Baltimore: Johns Hopkins University Press, 1993), is in favor of reading the Constitution in terms of principles, while Gordon Wood, *The Creation of the American Republic* (New York: Norton, 1973), does not view it as a document of principles. Bernard Bailyn, somewhere between the

two, sees the Constitution as an arrangement of institutions, laws and customs together with the principles which animated them. *The Ideological Origins of the American Revolution* (Cambridge: Harvard University Press, 1987).
4. *Constitutions of the States and the United States,* New York State Constitutional Convention Committee, 1938.
5. New York State Constitution, Art. XIV, § 1.
6. James Madison, as pivotal in the drafting of the Constitution as any, refused to publish his notes on the convention for the express reason that he himself did not want the Constitution to be understood in terms of specifics determined from the intentions of its authors.
7. U. S. Constitution, Art. III, § 2.
8. U.S. Constitution, Art. I, § 7.
9. Section III of the 1777 New York Constitution. See, generally, Dominic R. Massaro, "Foreordained Failure: NEW YORK'S EXPERIMENT WITH POLITICAL REVIEW OF CONSTITUTIONALITY," *New York State Bar Journal*, September/October 1998, 12.
10. In the last twenty years attention has been paid to rights granted and limitations imposed by the constitutions of the fifty states. The major impetus to the use of this approach was a law review article written by United States Supreme Court Justice William Brennan. Brennan, "State Constitutions and the Protection of Individual Rights," 90 *Harv. L. Rev.* 489 (1977).
11. Donald G. Morgan, *Congress and the Constitution. A Study of Responsibility.* (Cambridge: Harvard University Press, 1966).
12. Id. at 10.
13. Id. at 10-11.
14. See the discussion in chapter 6 on the efficacy of attempts by Congress to "overrule" the Supreme Court by postruling legislation.
15. Jesse H. Choper, *Judicial Review and the National Political Process/A Functional Reconsideration of the Role of the Supreme Court* (Chicago: University of Chicago Press, 1980).
16. 5 U.S. (1 Cranch) 137 (1803).
17. Thomas Jefferson, *The Complete Jefferson,* ed. Saul Padover (New York: Tudor Publishing Company, 1943), 123.
18. *Federalist 78* (Alexander Hamilton), in Alexander Hamilton, John Jay, James Madison, *Federalist Papers,* ed. Isaac Kramnick (New York: Penguin, 1987), 438-439.
19. 114 Cong. Rec. H 16,073 (June 5, 1968)
20. 1 Stat. 596 (1798).
21. History has demonstrated that the judiciary is as susceptible to war fever as the rest of society. For a more recent example of this fault, one need only refer to the decision of the Supreme Court upholding the internment of loyal Japanese-Americans, many of whom were citizens, following the attack on Pearl Harbor. *Korematsu v United States,* 323 U.S. 214 (1944).
22. This passage was omitted from the version of the Message which

was actually submitted to Congress. Morgan, *Congress and the Constitution,* at 403 n.1.
23. Jean Edward Smith, *John Marshall; Definer of a Nation* (New York: Henry Holt, 1996), 95.
24. 5 U.S. (1 Cranch) 137 (1803).
25. Leonard W. Levy, "Marbury v Madison," in *Encyclopedia of the American Constitution* (New York: Macmillan 1986), 3:1199.
26. *Marbury v Madison,* 5 U.S. (1 Cranch) 137 (1803).
27. *Fletcher v Peck,* 10 U.S. 87 (1810); *Martin v Hunter's Lessee,* 14 U.S. 304 (1816)
28. Paul Brest, "Legislation," in *Encyclopedia of the American Constitution* (New York, Macmillan 1986), 3:1142.
29. J. Richardson, ed., *Messages of the Presidents* (Washington: Government Printing Office, 1897), 6:9.
30. Roy P. Basler, ed., *The Collected Works of Abraham Lincoln* (New Brunswick, N.J.: Rutgers University Press, 1953), 2:401.
31. 358 U.S. 1 (1958).
32. Id. at 18.
33. Edwin Meese, "The Law of the Constitution," 61 *Tulane L. Rev.* 981, 983 (1987). That issue of the *Tulane Law Review* includes a symposium entitled "Perspective on the Authoritativeness of Supreme Court Decision" composed of articles attacking and analyzing Meese's approach.
34. Burt Neuborne, "The Binding Quality of Supreme Court Precedent," 61 *Tulane L. Rev.* 991, 999 (1987).
35. Paul M. Angle, ed., *Created Equal? The Complete Lincoln-Douglas Debates of 1858* (Chicago: University of Chicago Press, 1958), 36.

2 Children, Fear, and the Internet

1. E.g., *Bantam Books, Inc. v Sullivan,* 372 U.S. 58 (1963).
2. One can question whether this model ever was the norm in most homes, but it certainly was the perceived standard.
3. More recently, since most concerns regarding sexual issues as they relate to television and motion pictures have been mitigated for much of the populace, an additional concern about "excessive violence" has been expressed.
4. Quoted from Wesberry, *Every Citizen Has a Right to Know: A Report of the Georgia Literature Commission* (1954), 3, in Walter Gellhorn, *Individual Freedom and Governmental Restraints* (Baton Rouge: Louisiana State University Press, 1956), 55.
5. *Miller v California,* 413 U.S. 15 (1973).
6. *Ginsberg v New York,* 390 U.S. 629 (1968)
7. *New York v Ferber,* 458 U.S. 747 (1982).
8. *FCC v Pacifica Foundation,* 438 U.S. 726 (1978).
9. See, e.g., *Erznoznik v Jacksonville,* 422 U.S. 205, 211, 215 n. 13 (1975).

10. For example, the 104th Congress debated four bills relating to telecommunications reform, including the Telecommunications Competition and Deregulation Act of 1995, the Communications Decency Act of 1995, the National Education Technology Funding Corporation Act of 1995, and the Parental Choice in Television Act of 1995.
11. 103 Cong. Rec. S9746 (July 26, 1994).
12. S.314; 104 Cong Rec S1953 (February 1, 1995).
13. 104 Cong. Rec. S4841 (February 7, 1995)
14. These letters, as well as the further correspondence referred to below, are attached to the Declaration of Senator Patrick J. Leahy, filed in connection with *ACLU v Reno*, 929 F.Supp. 824 (E.D. Pa. 1996), aff'd 521 U.S. 844 (1997).
15. Chris Cox, "Surf's Up. The FCC Should Stay Out of It," *Roll Call*, October 23, 1995.
16. Hans A. Linde, "Due Process of Lawmaking," 55 *Neb. L. Rev.* 197, 223 (1976), referring to Julius Cohen, "Hearing on a Bill: Legislative Folklore," 37 *Minn. L. Rev.* 34 (1952).
17. The other plaintiffs in this action were Human Rights Watch, Electronic Privacy Information Center, Journalism Education Association, Computer Professionals for Social Responsibility, Clarinet Communications Corp., Institute for Global Communications, Stop Prisoner Rape, AIDS Education Global Information System, Bibliobytes, Queer Resources Directory, Critical Path AIDS Project, Inc., Wildcat Press, Inc., Declan McCullagh d/b/a Justice on Campus, Brock Meeks d/b/a Cyberwire Dispatch, and Jonathan Wallace d/b/a The Ethical Spectacle.
18. The other plaintiffs in the American Library Association suit were America Online, Inc., American Booksellers Association, Inc., American Booksellers for Free Expression, American Society of Newspaper Editors, Apple Computer, Inc., Association of American Publishers, Inc., Association of Publishers, Editors and Writers, Citizens Internet Exchange Association, CompuServe, Inc., Families Against Internet Censorship, Freedom to Read Foundation, Inc., Health Sciences Libraries Consortium, Hotwired Ventures LLC, Interactive Digital Software Association, Interactive Services Association, Magazine Publishers of America, Microsoft Corp., The Microsoft Network, L.L.C., National Press Photographers Association, Netcom On-Line Communication Services, Inc., Newspaper Association of America, Opnet, Inc., Prodigy Services Company, Society of Professional Journalists, and Wired Ventures, Ltd.
19. 438 U.S. 726 (1978)
20. *ACLU v Reno*, 929 F.Supp. 824 (E.D. Pa. 1996)
21. *Shea v Reno*, 930 F. Supp. 916 (S.D.N.Y. 1996)
22. *Reno v American Civil Liberties Union*, 521 U.S. 844 (1997)
23. 28 U.S.C. § 2412.
24. When Congress passes a law, any then-existing or future inconsistent

state law is "preempted," that is, overruled, by the federal law because of the Supremacy Clause of the U.S. Constitution. The issue is less clear when the preemption arises from the claim that Congress affirmatively determined not to legislate as to a subject. Thus the stated preemption clause in the CDA was intended clearly to demonstrate Congress's intent to be the sole legislative body regulating this form of Internet content.

25. Letter from Laura J. Murray, Director, Legislative Department, NYCLU, to Michael Finnegan, Counsel to the Governor, dated January 29, 1996, in the Governor's Bill Jacket, 1996 Chap. 600.
26. *People v Barrows*, 664 N.Y.S.2d 410 (Sup. Ct. Kings Co. 1997); 667 N.Y.S.2d 672 (Sup. Ct. Kings Co. 1998).
27. Both letters are found in the Governor's Bill Jacket, 1996 Chap. 600.
28. For the record, I should state that I am General Counsel of the Media Coalition.
29. McKinney's 1996 Session Laws of New York at 1900, 1901.
30. 42 U.S.C. §§ 1983, 1988.
31. *American Libraries Ass'n v Pataki*, 969 F. Supp. 160 (S.D.N.Y. 1997).
32. *Id.* at 170-171.
33. O.C.G.A. § 16-9-93.1
34. *ACLU of Georgia v Miller*, No. 96 CIV 2475-MHS (N.D. Ga., June 20, 1997)
35. See *People v Barrows*, 664 N.Y.S. 2d 410 (Sup. Ct. Kings Co. 1997); 667 N.Y.S. 2d 672 (Sup. Ct. Kings Co. 1998).
36. Borland, "Challenge to Net Porn Law Brews," *TechWeb News*, March 10, 1998.
37. Ibid.
38. Hal Rhodes, "Internet porn bill is costly grandstanding," *Albuquerque Journal*, March 6, 1998.
39. Conversation between the author and Steven Bunch, March 2, 1998.
40. 1998 New Mexico Laws, Chap. 64, codified as N.M. STAT. ANN. § 30-37-3.2(A)
41. Title XIV, § 1402(5).
42. Id. § 1402(4)
43. Id. § 1405(a), (c)(2).
44. The other plaintiffs were A Different Light Bookstore, ArtNet, The BlackStripe, Addazi, Inc. d/b/a Condomania, Electric Frontier Foundation, Electronic Privacy Information Center, Free Speech Media, LLC, Internet Content Coalition, OBGYN.NET, Philadelphia Gay News, PlanetOut Corporation, Powell's Bookstore, RIOT-GRRL, and Weststock.com.
45. *ACLU v Reno*, 31 F. Supp. 473 (E.D. Pa., 1999).

3 The Wright Brothers' First Plane Didn't Fly Either

1. Since I was actively involved in the Minneapolis and Indianapolis controversies about the MacKinnon/Dworkin ordinances and represented plaintiffs in the successful challenge of the Indianapolis ordinance, much of the material comes from my personal files. Much of the material is found in a form letter, with attachments, prepared by Charlee Hoyt early in 1984 to respond to inquiries concerning the ordinance ("Hoyt Letter"). A thorough discussion of the Minneapolis experience can be found in Donald Alexander Downs, *The New Politics of Pornography* (Chicago: University of Chicago Press, 1989).
2. *American Booksellers v Hudnut,* 598 F. Supp. 1316 (S.D. Ind. 1984), *aff'd* 771 F.2d 323 (7th Cir. 1985), *aff'd* 475 U.S.1001 (1986).
3. *Alexander v City of Minneapolis,* 531 F. Supp. 1162 (D. Minn. 1982).
4. Jean Bethke Elshtain, "The New Porn Wars," *The New Republic,* June 25, 1984, at 16.
5. Section I of Agreement for Services as Consultants to the Minneapolis City Council, Attachment F to Hoyt Letter.
6. Quoted in Downs, The New Politics of Pornography, at 79.
7. Ibid., at 80.
8. Ibid.,, at 61.
9. Letter, Laurence Tribe to Charlee Hoyt, January 8, 1984, quoted in David Bryden, "Between Two Constitutions: Feminism and Pornography," 2 *Constitutional Commentary* 180 (1985).
10. Letter from Laurence Tribe to Mayor Donald Fraser, May 1, 1984, quoted in Sanford Levinson, "What Do Lawyers Know (and What Do They Do With Their Knowledge)," 58 S. Cal. Law Rev. 441, 454 (1985).
11. Interesting issues are raised by the more general question of the extent and nature of the duties and obligations of the executive in executing and enforcing legislation it considers unconstitutional. While the uniquely executive aspects are not within the scope of this work, many of the issues and concerns are similar to those I discuss.. The exercise or nonexercise of the veto power is in many ways part of the legislative process. In that regard, the obligations and role of the executive with respect to constitutionality are similar to the of a legislator. Generally as to the appropriateness and limits of executive branch interpretation of the law, see Symposium, 15 *Cardozo L. Rev.* 21 (1993).
12. Letter from Robert J. Alfton, City Attorney, to Mayor Donald M. Fraser; George Caldwell, Director, Department of Civil Rights; and Joseph Kimbrough, Director, Minneapolis Library, dated February 23, 1984.
13. Letter from David M. Gross, Assistant City Attorney, to Mayor Donald M. Fraser; George Caldwell, Director, Department of Civil

Rights; and Joseph Kimbrough, Director, Minneapolis Public Library, dated March 27, 1984.
14. Downs, *The New Politics of Pornography*, at 113.
15. Ibid., at 120.
16. The quotations from the Administration hearing are taken from videotapes of the hearing prepared by the city government cable channel.
17. *Today Show*, NBC network, May 17, 1984.
18. E. R. Shipp, "Civil Rights Law Against Pornography is Challenged," *New York Times*, May 15, 1984, A14.
19. *American Booksellers v Hudnut*, 475 U.S. 1001 (1986).
20. The recent push by successful state defendants in § 1983 actions to recover fees and expenses under § 1988 may well demonstrate the wisdom of the generally applicable American rule.
21. *Civil Rights Organizing for Women v Douglas*, No. 22893-5-I, (Wash.Ct. of App., Div. 1 , September 30, 1988), denying a stay of the decision of the Superior Court of Whatcom County, No. 88-2-00965-8 (September 16, 1988).
22. *Village Books v City of Bellingham*, C88-1470D (W.D. Wash., February 9, 1989), reconsideration den. by order dated March 28, 1989.
23. Ibid.
24. From the Hoyt Letter.
25. 347 U.S. 483 (1954).
26. 163 U.S. 537 (1896).
27. The issues are considered in the context of advisory opinions in chapter 7 of this book.

4 A Constitution-Proof Law

1. *Nashville Tennessean*, June 26, 1977, 16A.
2. Larry Parrish, " Justification for Proposed Statutory Provisions" (undated, probably late 1977), 2.
3. Ibid. at 1.
4. Ibid. at 2.
5. " Bill's Author Vows It Will Wipe Out Obscenity," *Nashville Tennessean*, January 9, 1978, 9.
6. Ibid.; *Nashville Tennessean*, December 30, 1977, 12.
7. *Nashville Banner*, January 17, 1978, 17.
8. *Nashville Tennessean*, February 1, 1978, 1.
9. Tenn. Code Ann. § 8-6-101
10. Tenn. Code Ann. § 8-6-109(b)(5).
11. *Nashville Tennessean*, February 3, 1978, 1.
12. *Nashville Banner*, February 8, 1978, 15; *Nashville Tennessean*, February 8, 1978, 1.
13. *Nashville Banner*, March 1, 1978. 23.
14. *Nashville Tennessean*, March 5, 1978, 2B.
15. *Nashville Banner*, March 14, 1978, 1.

16. *Nashville Banner*, March 15, 1978, 12.
17. Ibid.; *Nashville Tennessean*, March 15, 1978, 1.
18. *Nashville Tennessean*, March 22, 1978, 1.
19. *Nashville Banner*, March 22, 1978, 1, 10.
20. *Nashville Tennessean*, March 30, 1978, 1.
21 *American Booksellers Ass'n v Leech*, Chancery Ct., Davidson Co., Tenn., Nos. 78-617-III, 78-709-III (July 7, 1979).
22. Id. at 1.
23. " Memphis Judge Voids State Obscenity Law," *Nashville Banner*, June 2, 1978, 15.
24. Mike Coleman, "Parrish to Appeal Obscenity Law Decision," *Nashville Banner*, July 8, 1978, 7.
25. At one point during the legislative history of the bill, Parrish threatened opponents of his bill with retribution at the polls by the religious and antipornography groups which he represented. While he subsequently retracted the threat, the pall from the original statement did not disappear.
26. *Leech v. American Booksellers Ass'n*, 582 S.W. 2d 738 (1979). Peggy Reisser, " State Court Voids '78 Obscenity Law," *Nashville Banner*, May 7, 1979, 1.
27. Ibid.
28. Editorial, " On Anti-Smut Measures, A Fine Line To Thread," *Nashville Banner*, May 9, 1979, 12.

5 If at First You Don't Succeed, Try, Try Again

1. *Furman v Georgia*, 408 U.S. 238 (1972).
2. See, e.g., Numan Bartley, *The Rise of Massive Resistance: Race and Politics in the South During the 1950s* (Baton Rouge: Louisiana State University Press, 1969); Louis Luski, "Racial Discrimination and the Federal Law: a Problem in Nullification," in *Southern Justice*, ed. Leon Friedman (New York: Pantheon, 1965); Harrel R. Rogers and Charles S. Bullock, *Law and Social Change* (New York: McGraw-Hill, 1972); and Francis M. Wilhoit, *The Politics of Massive Resistance* (New York: G. Braziller, 1973).
3. See, e.g., *Chandler v James*, 998 F. Supp. 1255 (M.D. Ala. 1997).
4. *Aguilar v Felton*, 473 U.S. 402 (1985), and *Grand Rapids School Dist. v Ball*, 473 U.S. 373 (1985).
5. *Bd. of Educ. v Wieder*, 72 N.Y.2d 174, 531 N.Y.S.2d 889 (1988).
6. McKinney's N.Y. Statutes, 1989, at 2429.
7. See, e.g., N.Y. Educ. Law § 314.
8. *Grumet v Bd. of Educ.*, 592 N.Y.S.2d 123 (3d Dept. 1992).
9. *Grumet v Bd. of Educ.*, 601 N.Y.S.2d 61 (Ct. of App. 1993).
10. *Bd. of Educ. v Grumet*, 512 U.S. 687 (1994).
11. Id. at 702, 703.
12. *Id.* at 703.
13. *Id.* at 717.

Notes to Pages 118–127

14. N.Y. State Finance Law §§ 123-a through 123-f.
15. *Grumet v Cuomo*, 625 N.Y.S.2d 1000 (Sup. Ct. Albany Co. 1995).
16. *Grumet v Cuomo*, 647 N.Y.S.2d 565 (3d Dept. 1996).
17. *Grumet v Cuomo*, 659 N.Y.S.2d 173 (Ct. of App. 1997).
18. 659 N.Y.S.2d at 178.
19. Joel Stashenko, "The Legislature Takes Another Shot at Creating Kiryas Joel District," *The Times Herald-Record (Orange County, N.Y.) Online Edition* (www.th-record.com), August 11, 1997.
20. Ibid.
21. Press release, "OU Welcomes Passage of Revised Kiryas Joel Legislation," August 4, 1997, Orthodox Union, Institute for Public Affairs.
22. "A Bad Law Breeds New Trouble," *New York Times*, April 6, 1998, A22.
23. *Grumet v Pataki*, Civ. No. 5648/97 (Sup. Ct. Albany Co., April 2, 1998); Joseph Berger, "Judge Rejects 3d Push to Keep School District of Kiryas Joel," *New York Times*, April 3, 1991, B1.
24. *Grumet v Pataki*, 675 N.Y.S.2d 662 (4th Dept. 1998).
25. *Grumet v Pataki*, 1999 N.Y. Lexis 1144 (N.Y. Ct. App., May 11, 1999).
26. Joseph Berger, "Court Decision Upsets School District Measure for Kiryas Joel," *New York Times*, May 12, 1999.
27. Joseph Berger, "Hasidic Village Has Few Ways to Get Own School District," *New York Times*, May 28, 1999. Joseph Berger, "Albany Tries Again to Aid Hasidic Village," *New York Times*, August 5, 1999.
28. McKinney's 1997 Session Laws of New York at 1938 and 2386.
29. *New York State Assembly Session Highlights 1997*, found at http://assembly.state.ny.us/Reports/Highlights/1997.
30. Press release, "OU Welcomes Passage of Revised Kiryas Joel Legislation."
31. 437 U.S. 402.
32. 117 S. Ct. 1997 (1997).
33. *Webster v Reproductive Health Services*, 492 U.S. 490 (1989).
34. Judy Mann, "A Battle in the War for Reproductive Rights," *Washington Post*, March 22, 1996, E 3.
35. Most of the history of this dispute is based on filings in the continuous litigation concerning Missouri family planning funding. *Planned Parenthood of Mid-Missouri and Eastern Kansas, Inc. v Dempsey*, Case No. 96-4186-CV-C-2 (U.S.D.C. W.D. Mo., Cent. Div., Gaitan, J.) (hereafter "Missouri Litigation").
36. James F. Wolfe, *"Abortion Foes Win 2 Battles,"* The Joplin (Missouri) Globe, *May 3, 1995.*
37. Undated declaration of Crystal Williams, in the Missouri Litigation (then known as *Planned Parenthood of Mid-Missouri and Eastern Kansas v Kivlahan*).
38. *Planned Parenthood of Minnesota v State of Minnesota*, 612 F.2d 359 (8th Cir. 1980), aff'd 448 U.S. 901 (1980); *Planned Parenthood of Central and Northern Arizona v State of Arizona*, 718 F.2d 938

(9th Cir. 1983); *Planned Parenthood of Kansas v City of Wichita*, 729 F. Supp. 1282 (D. Kan. 1990).
39. Rev. Stat. Mo. § 27.040.
40. Mann, "A Battle in the War for Reproductive Rights."; Amended Order, June 27, 1996, Missouri Litigation.
41. Amended Order, June 27, 1996, Missouri Litigation.
42. Will Sentell, "Politics Play Crucial Role in Funding Case," *Kansas City Star*, June 26, 1996, C1.
43. Memorandum of James S. Cole, General Counsel, Missouri Right to Life, January 2, 1997, filed in Missouri Litigation as Exhibit B to Declaration of Erika Fox dated June 27, 1997.
44. Sentell, "House Approves Plan to Limit Funds," *Kansas City Star*, May 21, 1997, C3.
45. An example of the effect of changing times and new technologies. Like the cable broadcasts of the Indianapolis City Council debates referred to in chapter 3, the Missouri legislative Internet dissemination not only opens the legislative debates to the public at large but also makes it possible for them to be memorialized.
46. Transcript in author's files.
47. Sentell, "State Funds Cut for Agency," *Kansas City Star*, May 23, 1997, A1.
48. Order of June 30, 1997, Missouri Litigation.
49. 137 F.3d 573 (8th Cir. 1998).
50. Joe Mannies, "Planned Parenthood, State Begin Another Court Fight Over Funding," *St. Louis Post-Dispatch*, June 23, 1998, B3.
51. *Planned Parenthood of Mid-Missouri and Eastern Kansas, Inc. v Dempsey*, 167 F.2d 458 (8th Cir. 1999).
52. Will Sentell, "Rules for Planned Parenthood OK'd," *Kansas City Star*, May 7, 1999, B1.

6 Legislative Reversal

1. Act of February 28, 1793, 1 Stat. 324; 2 U.S. (2 Dall.) 409 (1792).
2. *Chisholm v Georgia*, 2 U.S. (2 Dall.) 419 (1793).
3. A recent symposium entitled "The End of Democracy? The Judicial Usurpation of Politics" sponsored by and published in *First Things* (November 1996), included papers by former judge Robert H. Bork, Charles W. Colson, professors Russell Hittinger, Hadley Arkes, and Robert P. George. The symposium, organized by the Reverend Richard John Neuhaus, was, in many ways, emblematic of this mode of thought. Amid calls for a return to the Christian fundamentals allegedly underlying our system of government were straightforward renunciations of the role of the judiciary and calls for constitutional amendment and even direct resistance to institute rule by the legislative branch.
4. This discussion deals only with attempts to reverse decisions involving interpretations of the Constitution. When the Supreme Court rules

as to the meaning of a federal statute or another aspect of federal non-Constitutional law, it is clearly within both the power and the authority of Congress to pass a statute causing a contrary result.
5. 384 U.S. 436 (1966).
6. Controlling Crime Through More Effective Law Enforcement: Hearings Before the Subcomm. on Criminal Law and Procedure of the Senate Comm. on the Judiciary, 90th Cong., 1st Sess. 4 (1967) (hereafter "3501 Hearings").
7. 3501 Hearings, 2121.
8. Ibid.
9. 114 Cong. Rec. H 16,073 (1968).
10. *Michigan v Tucker*, 417 U.S. 433, 444-46 (1974).
11. Wright, *Federal Practice and Procedure—Criminal 2d* (1982), § 76 at 128.
12. 114 Cong. Rec. S 11595 (May 2, 1968); 114 Cong. Rec S 11740 (May 3, 1968); 114 Cong. Rec. H 16066 (June 5, 1968).
13. 114 Cong. Rec. S 11896 (May 6, 1968); Adam C. Breckenridge, *Congress Against the Court* (Lincoln: University of Nebraska Press, 1970), 79.
14. 114 Cong. Rec. S 12450 (May 9, 1968).
15. 3501 Report, 2137-28.
16. 3501 Report, 2133.
17. The following discussion is based, in part, on Eric D. Miller, "Comment: Should Courts Consider 18 USC § 3501 Sua Sponte?", 65 *U. Chi L. Rev* 1029, 1033-37 (1998).
18. Daniel Gandara, "Admissibility of Confessions in Federal Prosecutions," *Georgetown L.J.* 305, 311-12 (1974).
19. 114 Cong. Rec. S 12937-38 (May 13, 1968).
20. 115 Cong. Rec S 23236-38 (August 11, 1969).
21. *U.S. v Crocker*, 510 F.2d 1129, 1136-38 (10th Cir. 1975).
22. Miller, "Comment," at 1035.
23. Carrie Johnson, "A Lonely Crusade: Paul Cassell's Long-Running Assault on *Miranda* Finally Pays Off," *Legal Times* (February 15, 1999), 8.
24. *U.S. v Rivas-Lopez*, 988 F. Supp. 1424 (D. Utah 1997).
25. *United States v Dickerson*, 166 F.3d 667 (4th Cir. 1999).
26. 494 U.S. 872 (1990).
27. 117 S. Ct. 2157 (1997)
28. Id. at 2172.
29. See, e.g., "Bitter Over Ruling," *Washington Post*, June 26, 1997, A1.
30. Filed in 1998 as S.2148 in the Senate and H.R. 4019 in the House.
31. 494 U.S. 872 (1990).
32. *Sherbert v Verner*, 374 U.S. 398 (1963).
33. Nat Hentoff, "Is Religious Liberty a Luxury?" *Washington Post*, September 15, 1990 (referring to the views of Professor Laycock).
34. Religious Freedom Restoration Act of 1990, § 2(a)(4).
35. Id., § 2(b)(1).

36. Subcommittee on Civil and Constitutional Rights, September 27, 1990, 8.
37. Id. at 17.
38. Id. at 21.
39. Hearings on the Religious Freedom Restoration Act of 1990, Subcommittee on Civil and Constitutional Rights, House Judiciary Committee, September 27, 1990, 56.
40. Id. at 73.
41. Floyd Abrams, "Proposed Law Would Restore, Not Curb, Religious Liberty" *Legal Times*, March 30, 1992.
42. Bruce Fein, "Congress Takes Aim at State Sovereignty," *Legal Times*, March 16, 1992.
43. 103 Cong. Rec. S14469 (October 27, 1993).
44. Ibid.
45. 877 F. Supp. 335 (W.D. Tex. 1995).
46. 73 F.3d 1352 (5th Cir. 1996).
47. 117 S. Ct. 2157 (1997).
48. Id. at 2164.
49. Id. at 2185, 2186.
50. See, e.g., *In re Young*, 141 F.3d 854 (8th Cir. 1998). However, the dissenting judge disagreed. Id. at 863.

7 Advisory Opinions and Other Proposed Remedies

1. 104 Cong. Rec. S12468 (July 27, 1958).
2. *Langer v State*, 284 N.W. 238, 251 (N.D. 1939)
3. Charles Warren, *The Making of the Constitution* (New York: Barnes and Noble, 1967), 505, 506.
4. Robert P. Dahlquist, "Advisory Opinions, Extrajudicial Activity and Judicial Advocacy: A Historical Perspective," 14 *SW. U.L. Rev.* 46, n.15 at 51-52 (1983).
5. *Hayburn's Case*, 2 U.S. (2 Dall.) 409, 410 n.a (1792).
6. Charles Warren, *The Supreme Court in United States History* (Boston: Little, Brown, 1922), 1:108-111.
7. Id. at 110-111.
8. Warren, *The Supreme Court in United States History* (Boston: Little, Brown, 1922), 2:54-57.
9. H.J. Res. 317, 74th Cong., 1st Sess. (1935).
10. H.J. Res. 374, 74th Cong., 1st Sess. (1935).
11. H.J. Res. 344, 74th Cong., 1st Sess. (1935).
12. Discussed in chapter 1, at pp. 21–22.
13. Mel A. Topf, "The Jurisprudence of the Advisory Opinion Process in Rhode Island," 2 *Roger Williams L. Rev.* 207, 210 (1997).
14. Pub. Law 104-130.
15. Felix Frankfurter, "A Note on Advisory Opinions", 37 *Harv. L. Rev.* 1002-3 (1924).
16. Id., at notes 13, 14, and 15.

17. Donald A. Doernberg and Michael B. Mushlin, "History Comes Calling: Dean Griswold Offers New Evidence About the Jurisdictional Debate Surrounding the Enactment of the Declaratory Judgment Act," 37 *UCLA L. Rev.* 139 (1989).
18. Oliver P. Field, "The Advisory Opinion—An Analysis," 24 *Ind. L. Rev.* 203, 216 (1949).
19. Margaret M. Bledsoe, "The Advisory Opinion in North Carolina: 1947 to 1991," 70 *N.C. L. Rev.* 1853, 1862-1883 (1992).
20. William F. Swidler, ed., *Sources and Documents of the United States Constitution* (Dobbs Ferry, N.Y.: Oceana Publications, Inc., 1979), 10:52.
21. See, e.g., Bruce Allen Murphy, *The Brandeis/Frankfurter Connection* (New York: Oxford University Press, 1982).
22. R. Kennedy, "Advisory Opinions: Cautions about Non-Judicial Undertakings," 23 *U. Rich. L. Rev.* 173, 182, 190 (1989).
23. Frankfurter, "A Note on Advisory Opinions," note 266, at 1007.
24. Symposium, "The End of Democracy? The Judicial Usurpation of Politics," *First Things,* November 1996.
25. Edwin Borchard, *Declaratory Judgments,* 2d ed. (Cleveland: Banks-Baldwin Law, 1941), 87 ff.
26. Laws of 1915, c. 116, section 7.
27. Uniform Laws Annotated (St. Paul: West, 1996), 12:390 ff.
28. The present version is codified as 28 USC §§ 2201, 2202.
29. *Monroe v Pape,* 365 U.S. 167 (1961).
30. 2 U.S.C. § 692(a). Although both the House and Senate bills provided for a three-judge court as in the Communications Decency Act provision discussed later in text, it was deleted in conference.
31. 2 U.S.C. § 692(b).
32. 2 U.S.C. § 692(c)
33. P.L. 104-104, § 561, 110 Stat.142.
34. *Byrd v Raines,* 956 F. Supp. 25 (D.D.C. 1997).
35. *Byrd v Raines,* 521 U.S. 811 (1997).
36. It is interesting that the successor to the CDA, the Child Online Protection Act, passed in 1998, does not have an accelerated appeal provision.
37. We tend to forget that, while the trial was a public relations victory for the challengers of the Tennessee statute, Scopes was convicted. While the conviction was reversed by the Tennessee Supreme Court on a technicality, that court upheld the constitutionality of the law. At the same time, the court urged the state not to continue prosecution of Scopes, which advice was followed. The statute remained on the books, unenforced, for many years. Leonard W. Levy, Kenneth L. Karst, and Dennis J. Mahoney, eds., *Encyclopedia of the American Constitution* (New York: Macmillan, 1986), 3:1743.

8 Conclusion

1. In the survey conducted in conjunction with the writing of this book, as discussed in the appendix, 61 percent of the state legislators responding adopted this position, while 35 percent stated that they were obligated to follow the Constitution. Somewhat more surprising and troubling, 60 percent of the legal counselors (attorneys general, legislative counsel, and staff counsel) agreed that the will of the people superseded the constitutional oath.
2. Senator Carl Levin, a Democrat of Michigan, has described the process of drafting legislation in Congress:
   - A member has an interest or concern related to an issue. The member requests his/her staff to gather information.
   - The staff performs research that is coordinated with the member. During the research stage, the staff has many alternatives that can be used to gather information, including the Congressional Research Service (CRS) of the Library of Congress and its legal staff, Lexis/Nexis, the Internet, Senate Legal Counsel, the Senate Library, the Legislative Information Service database, and various interest groups and affected parties. During this stage, the constitutionality of any legislation being considered is reviewed and discussed.
   - Once the information is reviewed, the staff works with Legislative Counsel to draft proposed legislation. Legislative Counsel also has the opportunity to bring up any constitutional issues. The proposed draft is discussed and reviewed with the member. If the proposed draft bill has any constitutional implications, they generally are researched by CRS counsel, Senate Legal Counsel, and outside experts.
   - The bill is introduced and referred to the committee having cognizance over the proposed legislation. Committee staff research and scrutinize the language of the proposed legislation including the constitutionality of the proposed bill. Most frequently, any issues regarding the proposed legislation will be discussed at public hearings on the bill and with the Senator prior to markup. Before a bill is marked up and voted out of committee it undergoes additional review which would include constitutionality.
   - A committee report discusses any issues of constitutionality. The report is a public document that is prepared after markup and prior to the bill's consideration by the full Senate.

   Letter to the author, July 15, 1998. This states the paradigm of the process.
3. *Turner Broadcasting System, Inc. v FCC,* 117 S. Ct. 1174, 1189 (1997).
4. 47 U.S.C. § 231
5. Title XIV, § 1405(a), (b)

6. 47 U.S.C. § 1988.
7. 28 U.S.C. § 2412.

Statistical Appendix: *Analysis of a survey of Legislators, Legislative Counsels, and Offices of the Attorney General*

1. Donald G. Morgan, *Congress and the Constitution: A Study of Responsibility* (Cambridge: Harvard University Press, 1966).
2. Even in 1966, Morgan describes the plight of a legislator who declined to respond since his office was besieged with "1000 letters a day" (Morgan, *Congress and the Constitution*, at 366). Sadly, it would appear that innovations in communications technologies, such as the fax and e-mail, make it both more understandable and more excusable for the holders of political office to withhold their participation in studies such as this one. When calls were made to follow up the letters, not a few staff members indicated that participation in such studies was only considered in cases where the study was commissioned by a lobbying concern or conducted by a resident of the congressperson's home district.

    Most of the twelve responses came from members of Congress with well-defined ideological positions from both sides of the aisle: Allen (D-ME), Conyers (D-MI), Frank (D-MA), Gonzalez (D-TX), Gutknecht (R-MN), Kilpatrick (D-MI), Kolbe (R-AZ), Largent (R-OK), Oxley (R-OH), Petri (R-WI), and Slaughter (D-NY). One survey was returned anonymously.
3. Many states did not have legislative counsels or did not list them in the directory compiled by Leadership Directories, Inc., *State Yellow Book*, Winter 1997 (New York Leadership Directories).
4. To be sure, the data only "loosely" mirrors contemporary United States census data. New England is overrepresented, while the Middle Atlantic and Far West are underrepresented.
5. Morgan's geographic demarcations were maintained, despite their peculiarities, to allow for comparisons with his study.
6. One may speculate that this contributed to having had a lower rate of return on the federal side, though that would not explain the state experience. Of course, we have no control sample.
7. The question that was not included in the survey was solely federal,: "Are there any types of constitutional questions to which Congress should pay particular attention? (For example: conduct of foreign relations, federal-state relations, separation of powers, individual rights, non-justiciable questions, etc.)"

    Morgan, *Congress and the Constitution*, at 376.
8. "Legislators" includes only responses from legislators. "Counselors." includes only responses from attorney general's offices, legislative counsel and governor's counsel. "All" includes all responses. The percentages may not add to 100 because of rounding.
9. Morgan, *Congress and the Constitution*, at 10-11.

10. Unfortunately, Morgan is occasionally inexact when describing his findings.
11. Morgan, *Congress and the Constitution*, at 367-369.
12. In a political regime that ultimately rests upon its service to a single foundational document, those who can claim to best speak for the document occupy a position of supreme advantage. It was the Weimar, and later, Nazi, jurist, Carl Schmitt, who posed this issue in its most cynical terms. According to Schmitt, liberal constitutionalists obfuscate "the political"—the decision principle—by couching their very claims in such ostensibly unpolitical ways. Cf. Carl Schmitt, *The Concept of the Political*, trans. G. Schwab (Chicago: University of Chicago Press, 1996), and John P. McCormick, *Carl Schmitt's Critique of Liberalism* (New York: Cambridge University Press, 1997). Such deep cynicism undermines the common understandings necessary for the rule of law as well as for any meaningful normative distinctions between political regimes. In other words, political actors must be guided by a belief that they can adjudicate between claims based upon a single best interpretation, however provisional it may be. Cf. Jürgen Habermas, *Between Facts and Norms*, trans. W. Rehg (Cambridge: M.I.T. Press, 1996).
13. Morgan, *Congress and the Constitution*, 1 at 370.
14. This finding also challenges those thinkers, such as John Rawls, who give pride of place to the "public use of reason" within political institutions. Cf. John Rawls, *Political Liberalism*, (New York: Columbia University Press, 1993).
15. Morgan, *Congress and the Constitution*, at 371.
16. It is a misconception of their constitutional obligation for legislators, in determining the constitutionality of proposed legislation, to minimize the rulings of the Supreme Court.

Index

Abrams, Floyd, 159, 161
accelerated judicial review, 50, 186–189
ACLU v. Reno, 60, 61, 64
advisory opinions, 169–183
Agostini v. Felton, 123
Aguilar v. Felton, 123
ALA v. Pataki, 63, 64
Alabama, authorizing school prayer, 112
Alaska statehood, 3–4
Albuquerque Journal, 64
American Bar Association: Criminal Justice Section, 147; House of Delegates, 160–161
American Booksellers Foundation for Free Expression, 66
American Civil Liberties Union: challenge to CDA, 50–52, 175–176; challenge to COPA, 66; challenge to New Mexico internet content law, 64; challenge to New York internet content law, 58–59, 61; support of RFRA, 156
American Library Association, 50, 52, 58, 176
American Reporter, 50
Americans United for Separation of Church and State, 156
Arizona Constitution "English language only" provision, 13
Ashford, Charlie, 105
Atchley, Ben, 101–103, 104, 108
attorney generals, 101–104

Baker v. Carr, 158
Bank of the United States, 30
Bellingham, Washington, ordinance, 88–89
Biden, Joseph, 161
Blanton, Leonard Ray, 106
Bork, Robert, 182
Brandeis, Louis, 177
Brandt, Robert S., 107, 108
Brown v. Board of Education, 33
Bryan, William Jennings, 189
Bush, George, 161

California Constitution, length, 17
Cambridge, Massachusetts, proposition, 88
Campaign Life Missouri, 130
Canady, Charles T., 165
Carlin, George, 40, 50

Carnahan, Mel, 125, 134
Cassell, Paul, 153
Celler, Emanuel, 147
censorship as elitist, 38
Cherrick, Jordan B, 136
Child Online Protection Act (COPA), 65–66, 193
child pornography, 39–40
Choper, Jesse, 25
Citizens Against Pornography, 100
Citizens for Decency Through Law, 85, 100
City of Boerne v. Flores, 154, 163–164
Civil Rights Act of 1871, 87, 185–186, 196
Civil Rights Organizing for Women (CROW), 88
Clark, Ramsey, 151
Clinton, William J., 47, 154, 161, 173
Commission on Online Child Protection, 66, 193–194
Communications Act of 1994, 43
Communications Act of 1995, 47
Communications Decency Act, 42–53, 175–176, 187–189, 193, 195
constitutionalization of social and political issues, 10–11
Congress and the Constitution (Morgan), 22, 199
Cooney, C. Hayes, 102–103, 104, 106, 108
Cooper v. Aaron, 32
cost of litigation: impact on challengers, 11–13, 52–53; impact on government as defender, 12, 136; reimbursement of, 52, 87, 196–197
Coughenour, Beulah, 83, 86, 94
Council of Revision, New York, 22, 172
courts, politicization of, 10
Cox, Christopher, 47
Cuomo, Mario M., 114, 121
cynicism, creation of by irresponsible legislation, 13, 195–196

Daniels, Debbie, 94
Dannemayer, William E., 157
Darrow, Clarence, 189
Declaration of Independence, 16
Declaratory Judgment Act (U.S.), 185
declaratory judgments, 183–186
Deep Throat (film), 98
Diament, Nathan, 119
Dixon, Greg, 85
Dollinger, Richard, 119
Donnerstein, Edward, 85
Dornan, Robert, 161
Dred Scott decision, 34
Dworkin, Andrea: consulting agreement with Minneapolis, 75; proposed ordinance, 72–73. *See also* MacKinnon/Dworkin civil rights anti-pornography bill

Edwards, Don, 158, 159
Electronic Frontier Foundation, 50
Equal Access to Justice Act, 52, 196
Ervin, Sam J., 144, 145

Exon, Jim, 43, 45–46
Exon/Coats Amendment, 46–47

fact-finding, judicial, 49
FCC v. Pacifica, 50
Federalist 78, 26
Fein, Bruce, 160
Feingold, Russell D., 45, 69
First Amendment: CDA held to violate, 51; claim that New York internet content law violates, 57, 58; COPA held to violate, 66; Establishment Clause, 115; Georgia Computer System Protection Act held to violate, 62–63; Indianapolis, civil rights anti-pornography law held to violate 86–87; motion picture censorship, 35; Tennessee Obscenity Act of 1978 held to violate, 107
Ford, Gerald, 26, 146
42 USC § 1983, 87, 185–186
42 USC § 1988, 186
Frankfurter, Felix, 174–175, 177, 182
Fraser, Don, 78–79, 80–82, 85
Freedom to Read Foundation, 52

Gaffney, Edward, 159
Gaitan, Fernando J., Jr., 128, 129, 134, 135, 136
Georgia Computer System Protection Act, 62–63
Georgia Literature Committee, 38
Gingrich, Newt, 47
Gold, Emanuel, 119

Gorton, Slade, 43
Grassley, Charles, 161–162
Griswold, Erwin, 177
Gross, David, 75

Hamilton, Alexander, 26
harmful to minors. *See* obscenity as to minors.
Hatch, Orrin, 161, 162, 165
Hayburn's Case, 141
House, Ted, 133
House Judiciary Committee, Subcommittee on Civil and Constitutional Rights, 156
Hoyt, Charlee, 4–5, 74, 79, 83, 91
Hudnut, William, 83, 85, 86, 94
Hyatt, Al, 76
Hyde, Henry, 158–159

indecency, 40
Indianapolis, civil rights anti-pornography ordinance, 83–87; defeat in court, 86–87
Ingles, Stuart, 63
Institute for Public Affairs, Union of Orthodox Congregations of America, 119, 122
Internet: censorship, 41, 42–69; pervasiveness, 37
Internet Freedom and Family Empowerment Act, 47

Jackson, Andrew, 30–31
Jackson, Henry, 4, 167
Jacob, Ken, 133
Jay, John, 171, 181
Jefferson, Thomas: refusal to enforce the Sedition Act, 27–28; request for an advi-

Jefferson, Thomas (*continued*)
  sory opinion, 171, 181; view of the Constitution and its interpretation, 26, 31
Johnson, Gary, 64
Johnson, Lyndon B., 147, 151
Johnson, William, 172
judicial activism, 9, 53, 152–153
Judicial Conference of the United States, 147
judicial fact-finding, 49
"judicial monopoly" theory, 22–23, 81, 148–149
judicial review, 29–30

Kelley, Dean, 158
Kennedy, Anthony, 154
Kennedy, Edward, 161, 165
Kennedy, Robert, 182
Kiryas Joel, N.Y., School District, 112–124

Laycock, Douglas, 158, 159, 161
Leahy, Patrick J., 44–46, 69
legal "experts," 91–93, 97
legislative hearings: biased, 76–77, 89; impact of failure to hold, 49; lack of, 48, 76, 193; importance to legislative fact-finding function, 91, 192–193
Legislative Line Item Veto Act, 173, 187
legislative process, 48, 150, 192–193
Levy, Leonard, 28
Lincoln, Abraham, 32, 34
Linde, Hans A., 48

litigation, cost. *See* cost of litigation.
Lumbard, J. Edward, 150
Lupu, Ira, 159, 160

MacKinnon, Catharine: consulting agreement with Minneapolis, 75; proposed ordinance, 72–73; role in passage of Minneapolis ordinance, 75–78; role in passage of Indianapolis ordinance, 83–85. *See also* MacKinnon/Dworkin civil rights anti-pornography bill
MacKinnon/Dworkin civil rights anti-pornography bill, 4, 184–185
Mallory v. U.S., 144
Mansfield, Mike, 147
Marbury v. Madison, 3, 25, 28–30, 32, 154, 157
Marshall, John, 3, 28–29, 157, 172
McClellan, John, 145, 151
McGrath, David, 93
Media Coalition, 57, 64
Meese, Edwin, 33, 152
Memphis Leadership Foundation, 100
Minneapolis Civil Rights Office, 78
Minneapolis, proposed civil rights anti-pornography ordinance, 74–82
Miranda v. Arizona, 5, 118; attempts to reverse, 143–153
Missouri Catholic Conference, 125
Missouri family planning appropriations bills: FY

1993–94, 125; FY 1994–95, 125; FY 1995–96, 125–127; FY 1996–97, 128–129; FY 1997–98, 129–134; FY 1998–99, 134–136; FY 1999–2000, 137
Missouri Right to Life, 129
Mitchell, John, 152
Monroe, James, 172
Monroe-Woodbury Central School District, 113, 123
Moral Majority, 85
Morgan, Thomas C., 22–25, 199–201
Morse, Wayne, 147
motion pictures, sex and censorship, 35–36
Mull, J. Bazzel, 106

Nadler, Jerrold, 165
Nashville Banner, 105
National Conference of Commissioners on Uniform State Laws, 185
National Right to Life Committee, 160
National Writers Union, 50
Neuborne, Burt, 33
New Jersey declaratory judgment statute, 185
New Mexico Internet indecency law, 63–65
New York Civil Liberties Union, 54–57
New York Constitution: article XI, §3, 124; length, 17; process to amend, 90
New York Constitution of 1777, Council of Revision, 21–22
New York Internet indecency law: Senate Bill 210–D, 54–55; Senate Bill 210–E, 55–58, 61–62
New York State Court of Appeals: first Kiryas Joel decision, 115; second Kiryas Joel decision, 118–119; third Kiryas Joel decision, 120
New York State School Boards Association, 13, 115, 117, 118, 119, 123

Nixon, Jay, 128, 129, 135
Nixon, Richard M., 31, 151–152
North Carolina Supreme Court, 180

obscenity, as to minors (harmful to minors), 39–40, 59, 63
O'Connor, Sandra Day, 116
Omnibus Crime Control and Safe Streets Act of 1968, 5; §3501, reversing *Miranda*, 145–153
Oregon Employment Division v. Smith, 154, 155

Parrish, Larry, 97–98, 106, 107–109 proposed law, 98–100
Pataki, George, 54, 56, 57, 58, 199
People for the American Way, 156
Planned Parenthood Federation of America, 50
Planned Parenthood of Mid-Missouri and Eastern Kansas, Inc., 125–137
Preska, Loretta, 58–59, 61

Reems, Harry, 98
Religious Freedom Restoration Act (RFRA), 143, 153–166
Religious Liberty Protection Act, 154, 165
Reno, Janet, 45, 51, 161
Reynolds, David, 135
Roe v. Wade, 158

Safer Sex Page, 50
Salon Magazine, 66
Satmar Hasidim (sect), 113
Scalia, Antonin, 10
Schumer, Charles, 161
Scopes, John T., 189
Scopes "monkey" trial, 189
Sears, William R., 54, 56
Sedition Act, 27
Seidman, L. Michael, 11
Shaw (councilmember), 93, 94
Shea, Joe, 50
Smith, Christopher, 161
Solarz, Steven, 153, 157–158
Starr, Kenneth, 68
Starr Report, 68
Story, Joseph, 172
Strossen, Nadine, 159, 162
Supremacy Clause. *See* United States Constitution, Article VI (Supremacy Clause)
Supreme Judicial Court of Massachusetts, 177

Telecommunications Competition Act of 1996, 47
Telecommunications Competition and Deregulation Act (S.652), 44
television, 36

Tennessee District Attorneys General Conference, 101
Tennessee Legislative Joint Special Committee on Obscenity, 100
Tennessee Library Association, 106
Tennessee Obscenity Act of 1978, 101–106, 109 held unconstitutional, 107–108
Teresi, Joseph C., 120
test cases, 189–190
Traditional Values Coalition, 156
Tribe, Laurence, 79–81, 83, 85, 94
"tripartite" theory, 23–24
Tushnet, Mark, 11
Tydings, Joseph, 147

U.S. v. Wade, 144
Uniform Declaratory Judgments Act, 185
United States Catholic Conference, 160, 161
United States Constitution: Article III, 19, 170; Article VI (oath), 1; Article VI (Supremacy Clause), 18, 19, 136; Commerce Clause, 59, 61; First Amendment. (*see* First Amendment); Eleventh Amendment, 142; Thirteenth Amendment, 16; Fourteenth Amendment, 16; Fourteenth Amendment (Equal Protection Clause), 136; Fifteenth Amendment, 16; implementation of the Declaration of Independence, 16

United States Court of Appeals for the Eighth Circuit (Missouri family planning appropriations decision), 136
United States Court of Appeals for the Fourth Circuit (upholding §3501 of the Omnibus Crime Control Act), 152
United States Supreme Court: decision as to CDA, 51, 189; decision as to Kiryas Joel, 115; decision as to Line Item Veto Act, 188; decision as to MacKinnon/Dworkin ordinance, 87; decision as to RFRA, 64

University of Minnesota Law School, 72
Vermont Constitution, length, 17
Virginia Constitution of 1776, 181
Virginia Council of State, 28

Washington, George, 170, 171, 181
Wesberry, James Pickett, 38
Western Washington State University, 88
Wiggins, Harry, 127, 130
Wright, Charles Alan, 147
Wyden, Ron, 47